KARMIC MARKETING

Also by Dr. Joe Vitale

Faith
Expect Miracles
Zero Limits
The Miracle
The Art and Science of Results
The Fifth Phrase
The Abundance Paradigm

KARMIC MARKETING

The Most Magnetic Method for Attracting Wealth

Dr. Joe Vitale

Published 2021 by Gildan Media LLC
aka G&D Media
www.GandDmedia.com

Front cover design by David Rheinhardt of Pyrographx

Interior design by Meghan Day Healey of Story Horse, LLC

Library of Congress Cataloging-in-Publication Data is available upon request

ISBN: 978-1-7225-0312-3

10   9   8   7   6   5   4   3   2   1

To Percy Ross

Contents

Contents

Foreword

by Dan Strutzel

Throw away all of your assumptions about the old world of marketing, which were designed for a world of limited access to specific knowledge about a product or service. Forget about operating in a marketing world with high barriers to entry due to the high cost of direct mail, TV or radio ads, catalogs, or billboards. That world no longer exists.

In today's digital economy, intelligent technology provides detailed product information with one click, or even delivers that information directly to the consumer in an automatically personalized form.

Marketing can no longer rely on gambits that seem inauthentic or dishonest. In this new world, the consumer knows almost as much as you do about your product. Competitors can easily compete with your marketing efforts, thanks to a low barrier to entry on the Internet. You must step up your game.

The world has evolved, and as a marketer operating in this new world, you must evolve with it. We have entered an era where trust determines whether your marketing efforts will be successful.

According to Joe Vitale, there is no more effective method for gaining that trust than *karmic marketing*.

In this book, Joe will describe karmic marketing and show how it operates differently from its traditional equivalents. He'll discuss the core principles of karmic marketing as well as the secrets of karmic marketing masters. You'll get a short course on the greatest money-making secrets in history, hypnotic publicity secrets, karmic marketing methods for your website, email, and social media, the future of marketing, and more.

Joe is the author of numerous books, notably *The Attractor Factor: Five Easy Steps for Creating Wealth or Anything Else from the Inside Out*, which was twice a number one best seller, and *Zero Limits: The Secret Hawaiian System for Health, Wealth, and Peace*.

Joe certainly knows how to market himself well. He was one of the stars of the hit movie *The Secret*, and he has been on TV shows including *Larry King Live* and *Extra*. He wrote the only book on the business secrets of the nineteenth-century marketing genius P. T. Barnum, entitled *There's a Customer Born Every Minute*. Known for his outrageous publicity stunts, Joe received local and national attention from media such as the *New York Post* for the world's first canine concert in order to promote that best-selling book. He's also written *Hypnotic Writing* and *Buying Trances: A New Psychology of Sales and Marketing.* Joe has been called the Buddha of the Internet.

Joe knows what he's talking about when it comes to marketing. His methods have made people millionaires. He's been involved with every aspect of marketing from traditional direct mail to publicity to infomercials, and he's the president of Hypnotic Marketing, Inc.

This book will provide you with Joe's most cutting-edge material on marketing. Many of its ideas that follow have never been discussed by him publicly.

Karmic Marketing will show you how to establish a greater level of trust between you and your customers. You'll learn how to cut through the noise and stand apart from the crowd (especially in the overcrowded online world). You'll make your marketing simpler and clearer, leading to a more balanced and less stressful life for you. Perhaps most importantly, you'll gain a greater sense of fulfillment, knowing that you are not just selling products and services but making a difference in your customers' lives.

Introduction

by Joe Vitale

I've been mentioning karmic marketing for a decade or more. It's high time that I explain what it means. Here's a quick definition:

Karmic Marketing is *giving now, knowing that in some way, shape, or form, you will be getting later.*

Here's how it works:

You're rewarded instantly when you give because of the good feelings you get. Those feelings act like magnetizers that will attract more good feelings.

You're rewarded later because of the invisible law that says you will get from giving.

I looked at this topic in my books *The Greatest Money-Making Secret of All Time* and *Life's Missing Instruction Manual*, but I didn't discuss it from a karmic marketing perspective. So let me give you an example or two:

One weekend I gave everyone a copy of the DVD of Rhonda Byrne's best-selling film *The Secret*. I bought the DVDs out of my own pocket. I didn't ask for, or expect, any money for them. I gave from my sincere desire to share.

Later that same night I received an email from Rhonda. She said she was sending me, as a gift, a box of fifty DVDs of the movie.

That's almost twice as many DVDs as I gave out.

That's karmic marketing.

At one point during the same event, I used a magic trick to turn a roll of Life Savers into a hundred-dollar bill and gave it to an astonished woman in the audience.

I didn't ask for anything in return.

Two days later, that same woman asked me a question in front of everyone that let me plug my next Beyond Manifestation weekend. That plug led to my making $2,000 in one minute.

That's karmic marketing.

The idea is to give freely, from your heart, wanting to share and wanting to help, and not expecting anything in return from the people you are doing it for. You simply trust that your good deed will in time come back to you tenfold in some surprising and wonderful ways.

I practice karmic marketing on the Internet by giving people things that I believe they will love, such as an e-book, a course, an audio, or a coupon.

On one level, it strengthens our relationship.

But on the unseen level, it starts a spiritual circulation. My giving now—done from my heart, with no expectation from the people I am doing it for—leads to getting later.

Karmic marketing is not done often, because too many people are into survival. They are afraid to let go. To trust. They are desperate, and they stay desperate because of this lack of trust in life. But once you let go and trust, you step into a flow that is prosperity itself.

My blog is karmic marketing at work. I write posts about whatever I want, doing my best to entertain, educate, inspire, and inform. No one pays me for this. I could make more money writing a sales letter or a book or creating a website.

What comes to me as a result of writing my blog?

Increased business.

Increased sales.

Increased fans.

Sometimes an Amazon gift certificate.

But I'm not doing it for the end result.

I'm doing it because I want to.

Because I love to.

Because I love *you*.

Ao Akua

1
The Power of Karmic Marketing

Marketing redirected and improved my life, gave me abundance, and provided me with immeasurable success.

How did that come about? I did not know what marketing was as I was beginning my journey of being a published author. My goal was just to be an author. I wanted to create things that made a difference in people's lives. I wanted to make them happy through my written work.

It took a long time for my first book to be published. It came out in 1984. It was called *Zen and the Art of Writing*.

It was a glorious moment, because after decades of struggle, I was finally published. But it was also one of the most disappointing moments of my life, because I realized that publishers don't know how to market books. In general, they're nothing more than glorified printers.

Although I was published, nobody knew it but me and my family. That began the mad scramble of getting my book noticed.

That's when I started to explore marketing. I discovered that there were things called advertising, publicity, direct mail, direct media, and direct marketing. I dived in headfirst, because I wanted to know the secrets of promoting a product, namely my own.

I learned the hard way: by going to the library, reading all the books, and applying everything I was reading. Before you knew it, I started to sell my own book. My publisher couldn't do it. Nobody else was doing it. But I started to do it in my own way, barely understanding what I was doing.

As I started to sell my book, people started to notice, and they would write to me.

This is 1984, before the Internet. I'm really struggling. I'm still in poverty in Houston. But people are finding out that this Joe Vitale guy has a book coming out. How's he getting it noticed?

A lot of those people were struggling authors and speakers who wanted to be noticed. I said, "It's marketing.

I've learned how to write sales letters and news releases and send them out to the media."

These people wanted to know how to market their books, so I began as a marketing consultant. Then they wanted me to market *their* books, so I began as a copywriter. In short, I applied everything I learned about marketing to myself.

I was my first client. As the book did well and people noticed it and started hiring me, I pulled out of poverty, because I was now making money as a marketer. Because I was thinking as a marketer, I wrote a book called *Hypnotic Writing*, which was born out of the idea that I needed another product besides the first one. Because I knew publishers didn't really know what they were doing, I published it myself.

This was back in the late eighties and early nineties, when Kinko's was the neighborhood printing shack. I would print off my own copies and sell them through the marketing practices that I was learning.

That's how marketing has changed my life. It's still changing my life as I apply it in different ways.

Today we have more technology. We have the Internet. We have apps. We have social media. We have things we'd never dreamed of. Even the science fiction writers of the last century didn't dream of some of the things we now take for granted. But in my book on P. T. Barnum, *There's a Customer Born Every Minute*, I pointed out ten things that Barnum did that we can still do today.

In short, there are basic principles that always work. It doesn't matter what the time frame is.

On his deathbed, Barnum said he owed his fame and fortune to the newspapers of the world. The newspapers ran his stories. How did they know what the stories were? He was practicing good marketing, and he was telling them.

We still do the same thing today. It's a marketing technique to use publicity. The only difference is instead of having to call, visit, or send a telegram or snail mail letter to a media person, now you can do it instantaneously by email or social media.

What, then, is marketing?

My own definition of marketing is everything that is done to bring attention to your product or service. It's an umbrella term that can cover everything from advertising, publicity, and trade shows to cold calling, email campaigns, and much more.

Karmic marketing is a subject I've wanted to write about since the last century. I have occasionally talked about it, and people would raise their eyebrows, but I never really explored it or explained it. Yet it's been the secret to my success. I've created a small business empire based on karmic marketing.

I purposely named it *karmic marketing* because it's an unusual name. I knew it would make people curious and want to know more.

Karmic comes from *karma*, a Sanskrit word that basically means *action*. Although it's often used in a religious context, I'm not talking about religion. I'm talking about cause and effect.

Karmic marketing is an action you take to get a result that you desire. In this particular case, we're really talking about giving, which I want to explore in depth, because it goes beyond all the marketing anybody has ever heard of before. It goes into the psychological, into the metaphysical, maybe even into quantum physics, because we're talking about performing an action—karma—that leads to a desired result that is related to our product or service. Karmic marketing is a way to take an action to market you, your product, or service.

Marketing has always been with us, although it wasn't called that in the early days. There's evidence of marketing from the Roman town of Pompeii back in 35 BC. The city was known for a popular fish sauce called *garum*, which was like the fish sauce used today in Asian cooking. There are many images that were used to advertise it, and a number of them have survived to the present.

In the sixteenth century, *marketing* as a word started to be used to describe driving people to the marketplace. It wasn't until 1897 that marketing the way we understand it today—as a way to move goods using sales and advertising—came into common understanding.

Marketing generally means anything that you do to bring attention to your business. Before you actually sell your product or service, you've got to get attention for it, which is usually done through marketing.

Marketing goes way back. I discovered that in London in the 1800s, people would put ads on the back of gravestones. On the front was the name and dates of the deceased. On the back was, say, "Buy Jones' soap." Later the practice was discontinued on the grounds that it was disrespectful.

In any case, different ways of marketing have been around for a long time, probably going back to the beginning of human history.

Many people have negative associations with marketing. I've often heard from entrepreneurs who say, "I don't like marketing. It's obnoxious. I don't feel good doing it." When I first heard this, it concerned me, because I thought, "It's essential to your business. You have to do it or hire somebody to do it."

Then it dawned on me. These people were thinking about marketing in the old-school sense of tricking people. You would lie to people and mislead them. You could get away with it then, because there weren't the legalities to control what you were saying. P. T. Barnum was often called a huckster, but he was actually pulling practical jokes on people in order to draw their attention to his product or service. He did it in a good-natured way, so it was fun.

Some people say they don't like marketing and selling because they're associating these things with the taint of the past, so I've reinterpreted the concept. I say it's sharing—sharing your love, your passion, and your devotion to your product or service.

Decades ago, I had a massage therapist. Usually when I got a massage, she was very quiet. But this particular time, she wouldn't stop talking. She had seen a movie the night before, and she loved it. The film moved her so profoundly that she had to tell everybody, including her clients, who were paying for silence. I realized that she was marketing the movie. She would not call it that, but she was raving about something she truly loved. Because she raved about it, she awoke an interest in me, and I went to see it. Later on, I even ended up meeting the director.

In essence, you're selling something that hopefully you believe in. If you truly believe in it, then share your enthusiasm. Share it with sincerity. Share it with the story that got you excited in the first place.

That is the marketing of today. People want authenticity. People want enthusiasm. People want sincerity. When you are genuinely moved by your own product or service, you naturally talk about it. An organic sales and marketing process takes place. The old, primitive way of manipulating people falls away, because you're coming from your heart. Now it's more heart-centered, and getting closer to what I call karmic marketing.

That much said, marketing techniques that were being practiced back in the eighties and nineties are still being used today. Traditional media—newspapers, magazines, they're still around. Television, radio—are all still around, and they're all starving for stories. Your business, your product, your service, you yourself are all stories that could be funneled to them.

One technique that was being used back in the last century and is still used today is direct mail. Direct mail is powerful. Some marketing legends, like Dan Kennedy, who has deeply influenced me, swear by it. Actually, it's even more powerful today, because most of your competition isn't using it.

Direct mail is writing a powerful sales letter and mailing it to a target audience. If you really hit with a match between the right audience and the right offer, you can strike gold. That's still true, but fewer people are doing it, because they move everything online. They think, "Instead of paying for postage and printing, why don't I pay for a website and do an email campaign?" That's wonderful, but that should be just one aspect of your marketing rather than the sole thing you do.

Many people are saying advertising doesn't work. Of course advertising still works. That's why people are spending so much money on ads, whether they're in magazines and newspapers or on television. Advertising is very powerful.

My first taste of television impact was in the early 1990s. One of my clients had an infomercial, and he wanted me to write copy for it. He also put me in the infomercial. He just wanted me to walk to my mailbox and show me pulling out some envelopes, implying that I was getting checks in the mail, and walk back to the house. That's all I did. No speaking role. I had nothing to do with the product or service otherwise.

Nonetheless, I noticed that after the infomercial aired, everybody recognized me. They'd walk up on the street and say, "I saw you in the show last night."

I thought, "What show? I wasn't in any show." They'd seen the ad. I realized that television—then and now—is one of the most persuasive marketing tools of all time.

All of the old media are still around, and they're still valid means of marketing. Many things haven't changed. You still have to know what you're doing. You still have to test. You still have to have a great offer. You still have to have a great product. When everything falls in the line, bingo! It's like a lotto win.

Many people say, "I would do a billboard or a television ad if I had the money." That's actually an excuse. You don't need more money. You need more creativity.

When you say we need money in order to put up a billboard, take out an ad, or run a TV commercial, you're falling for one of the oldest tricks in the book. It is self-sabotage. On one level, everybody's got to agree with you: you really need money, because those media are expensive. You'll feel good because you've got other people that are in the victimhood mentality with you, and you don't feel alone.

But I've been around the block a few times. I know that if you get creative, you can create relationships that enable you to get what you're going for; you can accomplish your big goals even without money.

Karmic marketing is pointing in that direction, because it involves giving. Because your giving is done in a specific way that I'm going to explain, you'll trigger a reaction from the public and, if you want to get metaphysical, from the universe itself.

This reaction is going to bring you benefit. It could be in the form of cash. It could be in the form of opportunities. It could be in the form of expanded business. It could be in the form of new partners. It could be in the form of something I can't even imagine.

Become aware of your limiting beliefs and the possibility of self-sabotage.

When I was copywriting, I would chisel my sales letters. I would put in everything I'd learned from my own creativity, from all of my mentors, books, and everywhere else. I would pour myself into the letter.

I would give my copy to the client, who would look at it and change something. In their mind, they were improving it, but unconsciously it was a form of self-sabotage. The changes made the copy worse. They made it not work.

When this first happened, I thought, "Why would this client hire me and then change what I did?" It made no sense to me until I started to look at it from the perspective of beliefs. If somebody has the belief that they don't deserve success, they will sabotage their own success because they are unconsciously afraid of it. They may say, "I changed the headline because my wife said it would be stronger this way" or "I changed the postscript because I didn't feel comfortable with it." But that's just a smoke screen, a rationalization for a self-sabotage maneuver.

As a result, I began to focus more on beliefs, because I realized that I can't teach anybody marketing if they still believe they don't deserve success or that money is evil.

A similar belief, which I've already mentioned, is that marketing is manipulative. Marketing is obnoxious. Marketing is shady. Marketing is dark. Marketing is evil. Marketing is lying.

Old-school marketing—back in the 1800s, when they were putting ads on the backs of tombstones—was probably dark and manipulative, but it's not present-day marketing.

Sometimes people will say, "I need to market to everybody, because everybody needs this product or service." No, not everybody needs your product. You need a tight market, a niche. It might be a large group, it might be a small group, but the right niche can make you wealthy if you target it right.

People say, "Marketing doesn't work. Advertising doesn't work. Publicity doesn't work." All this means is that they tried something in these arenas that didn't work, and they didn't go back to the drawing board and retry. Many old-school marketers had to keep running ads and tweaking them until they hit on the exact combination that would get a result. When they hit on that combination, they would stay with it. Somebody today thinking, "Advertising doesn't work, marketing doesn't work, publicity doesn't work," is shooting themselves in the foot, because they haven't tried hard enough or hired the pros that could help them succeed.

Karmic marketing is completely different from these methods. It is based on the idea that there is a benevolent universe—call it what you want: the God, the Divine, the cosmos. If you're an atheist, you can just call it nature. In any case, there is an ebb and flow in the circulation of the world. When you practice karmic marketing in the way that I will explain, you put into action a particular way of being and doing that brings you the results you want.

As I've said, traditional marketing still works. You can think of karmic marketing as giving a turbo boost to traditional types. Karmic marketing makes them much more effective. It moves you in the direction of being open to the success you want. If you give in a certain specific way, it will trigger reception on your part. Because you have dropped your limiting beliefs, you will be able to receive what's coming your way. If you add karmic marketing to whatever you're already doing, it's going to double or triple your results, maybe even increase them by a factor of ten.

As I've already pointed out, if you have negative beliefs about yourself, success, money, or marketing, what you implement will backfire. As you clear up those beliefs, you will enable yourself to receive the riches you've been longing for and actually deserve.

Let me give an example of how karmic marketing worked for me. In the 1990s, I came out with a book called *Spiritual Marketing*. I was learning marketing and becoming known as a copywriter, but I always had a spiritual side to me; I was always practicing what I called spiritual marketing. I wrote a little booklet with that title—it was only about twenty pages long. I printed it, folded it, stapled it, and called it a book.

I wrote this book for my sister, who was struggling at the time. She was on welfare and trying to raise three kids. I thought, "She needs to know some of the things I've learned about spirituality, marketing, and metaphysics," so I dedicated *Spiritual Marketing* to her. I gave it to her; she read it and implemented it. It worked. She got off welfare and raised her kids. She made a difference in her life.

Occasionally when I met somebody that seemed open-minded, I'd give them a copy of *Spiritual Marketing*. At one point, self-help author Bob Proctor invited me to an event he was holding on the science of getting rich in Denver. Because he was giving me free admission, I gave him a copy of *Spiritual Marketing*. I just said, "Here's an unpublished book. I thought you might like it." He not only liked it but stood on stage in front of 250 people and said, "Joe Vitale's in the room. He's written a book called *Spiritual Marketing* and you're all going to want it."

I was embarrassed. I said, "I don't have a book. This isn't done. This isn't published." At the break, 250 people stampeded me, including a publisher.

Meanwhile, I had put the book online for free. Something in me said, "Just give it away." I remember wrestling with the idea. Many people would have said, "Put it on a website, but get their email address. You can build a database that you can mail to." Which is a very valid marketing technique, and one I teach. But I didn't use it for *Spiritual Marketing*.

Because I gave that book away, about five million people got it. Because Bob Proctor talked about it on stage, that publisher published the book basically sight unseen. It was an early print-on-demand (POD) book, meaning there was no warehouse full of books; they were being published as people bought them. It became my first Amazon best seller.

Because of all of this attention, *The New York Times* wrote a story about POD books and featured *Spiritual Marketing*. Then, thanks to that article and the Internet buzz, a major publisher, John Wiley, called me and said, "We want to publish your book. We don't like the title *Spiritual Marketing*, but we like your platform. We like you. We like the buzz you're getting."

I ended up retitling *Spiritual Marketing* as *The Attractor Factor*, which has become the number one best seller of all the eighty-plus books I've written.

The story doesn't end there. A woman in Australia was given a copy of *The Attractor Factor*. She read it and called me up. She said she was a movie producer, and she wanted to make a movie about the law of attraction. She wanted me to be in it.

I hemmed and hawed. Although I had been on TV for my P. T. Barnum book, I hadn't been in a movie. But I was smart enough to say, "Yes, if you get it together, give me a call."

The producer did get it together. She flew me to Chicago, and she filmed me for what became one of the most influential movies of all time, *The Secret*, which threw me into outer space in terms of fame and fortune. It put me on *Larry King Live* twice. Oprah did three infomercial-type messages for it. I made many radio and television appearances and started traveling around the world. Book deals became even easier.

All of this success came from karmic marketing. I wrote *Spiritual Marketing* and gave it away. I didn't even require an email address. Because I put this book out as a gift to the world, it started coming back in ways I could never have predicted.

The success that comes from karmic marketing is bigger than you imagined and arrives in unexpected ways. You can't orchestrate or strategize those connections. I could not have sat back in the 1990s and said, "I'm going to write this little book. A good strategy would be to give it away; then maybe some influencer, like Bob Proctor, will pick it up. Maybe there'll be a publisher there, and maybe *The New York Times* will do a story. Maybe a publisher will call me afterwards and get me on Larry King. Maybe a woman in Australia will make a movie that makes an impact, so it will all pay off in the end."

I could not have created a strategy that would accomplish any of those things. But karmic marketing did.

2
The Core Principles

want to delve deeper now into the core principles of karmic marketing.

The Principles of Karmic Marketing

1. Karmic marketing is giving now, knowing that in some way, shape, or form you will be getting later.

2. The hole you give through is the same hole through which you will receive.

3. Karmic marketing rewards you instantly through the good feelings you get.

4. Karmic marketing gives freely from the heart, wanting to share and help, and not expecting anything in return from those you are giving to.

5. Karmic marketing is built on a foundation of trust, giving, and being detached from outcomes.

6. Karmic marketing operates on two levels: the seen and the unseen.

7. Karmic marketing is most effective when it is infused with what the practitioner loves or is passionate about.

Principle number one: karmic marketing is giving *now*, knowing that in some way, shape, or form you will be getting *later*. As my own experience has shown, when you give in the way that I recommend, you will probably receive, in an unexpected way, many times what you gave, usually tenfold. It will come in its own good time.

On one level, this is simply a feel-good philosophy, but it becomes your reality when you practice it with an expectation of success. Because beliefs rule the earth, life is an optical illusion. As a result, you get what you believe. If you think, "Karmic marketing doesn't work. If I give, I'll just have less," you will prove that to yourself, because your belief will become a self-fulfilling prophecy. You will make it so in order to be right.

By the same token, if you act according to the new belief that the more you give now, the more you will receive later in some unexpected ways, you will prove that, because the belief is operative. Whatever we believe, we are going to create.

Let me give you an example. Years ago, when I discovered that beliefs were operating in everybody, including me, I decided to create a new belief about how I spent money. I created a belief that the more money I spent, the more I would receive.

That sounds false, like a simpleton's way of trying to live through rationalizing. "You spend some money, thinking you're going to get more as a result? That's a fool's game."

But I started to notice that the more money I spent, the more money started to show up. It isn't unlike me to buy something in the morning and in the afternoon find a check or a bank wire for the amount I just spent, or more.

I started saying this during seminars. Once a tax attorney came up afterwards. I thought, "Oh, boy. Here we go. He's going to slam me, because we know what he thinks about that. For him, spending is a deduction, a subtraction. You don't get more money when you spend money."

But the attorney walked up and said, "You're correct."

I said, "I am?"

"Yes, the more money you spend, the more you will receive, if that is your mindset."

When I say that when you give now, you will receive ten times or more that amount, on one level it's a new belief. But as you buy into that belief, it becomes your new reality. It is real.

Some people fear that if they give too much, they will be taken advantage of. What's far more important from a karmic marketing standpoint is your mindset when you give. I'm talking about a trusting faith-based perception that what I give now is going to come back to me in some way, shape, or form in an unexpected way, ten times or more.

When you have that mindset, your receiving does not depend on whom you give to. Bob Proctor once said that when he gives money to somebody, he doesn't care if they burn it, if they spend it, if they invest it, if they are self-destructive with it. It is not in his hands once he passes it along.

Karmic marketing needs to have the same perspective. If you're saying, "I'm going to give now because I want to get," that's the wrong philosophy. You're giving now, knowing it's going to come back to you, but not knowing how or by whom.

If somebody is giving to a person or institution that they expect to be the source of their return, they're not practicing karmic marketing, because they're trying to control the process. Their ego is saying, "I gave to this customer, so this customer needs to give back." No. Karmic marketing is giving products, services, or money to your source of spiritual nourishment, knowing that it will come back to you multiplied in some unexpected way, but not necessarily from that same source.

Principle two: the hole you give through is the same hole through which you will receive. The bigger you make the hole for giving, the bigger the reward you will receive.

It's like a window. If it is only cracked open a little bit so that you can slide a dollar through it, it can only receive the same amount. But if you open the window entirely and put a bushel of $100 bills through, that window is now open to receive bushels of $100 bills. The bigger you make that hole for giving, the bigger the hole will be for receiving.

Principle three: karmic marketing rewards you instantly through the good feelings you get. They act like magnetizers that attract more good feelings. From a metaphysical point of view, we attract what matches our vibrations—meaning our emotions and our energetic makeup. If somebody is feeling sad or depressed, when they look into the world, they are likely to see things that are sad and depressing, and their future moments are going to match the ones that they're experiencing.

It behooves us metaphysically and psychologically to raise our vibration to feel better. There are many different ways to accomplish this: exercise, drinking more water, swimming, dancing, movement, getting sunshine. Karmic marketing is another way.

I know a young man in Thailand named Andres Pira. He started out homeless, but he is a billionaire at the age of thirty-six. (I helped him write a book called *Homeless to Billionaire.*) He credits his success in part to what he calls *vibrational giving.* This is a kind of tangent to karmic marketing. Andres points out that the very act of giving changes you psychologically and chemically. It changes your whole biology. He calls it *vibrational giving* because the giving raises your vibration.

Another example is an inventor in Austin, Texas, named Terry Jones, who invented an exercise device called a Nexersys, which is like a computerized sparring partner. It costs a few thousand dollars, but it has been a big hit.

Terry gave me a Nexersys when he first developed it many years ago. He brought it to my house and put it together in my gym. He asked nothing in return. Then a couple of years ago, when I was going through a divorce and I no longer had access to that Nexersys, he brought me another one. He came to the house with his son, and they put it together. Terry said, "It's yours."

I stared at him, saying, "This is a big gift."

Recently I followed up with him. I asked, "Terry, you gave me two Nexersyses. Why? What was your motivation? Were you hoping for publicity from me? Were you hoping for me to talk about it on social media?"

"No," he said. "I gave because it felt fantastic to give."

Notice that Terry did not ask anything of me. He did not ask for a testimonial. He did not ask me to appear in a TV commercial or on social media. He gave two of those systems to me free and clear. As a result, he did feel better. His vibe went up.

Actually, I did make a Nexersys video for social media. I was also interviewed by an Austin newspaper, and I gave it a glowing review. And of course I'm talking about the Nexersys in this book.

But Terry did not give to get those results. He gave for that feeling of instant satisfaction. Maybe on some level he felt, "I'm going to give now. It feels great to give now. In and of itself, the giving is complete. But maybe it will also influence my business in some way down the road." And it has.

Traditional marketing often has an air of desperation about it. It's like going to Vegas and playing craps. The marketer is saying, "I'm putting everything on this ad. It had better work." Then they roll the dice, and if the ad doesn't do well, they plummet. They are not happy. They don't feel good. They feel they've failed. That then influences the next decision.

Karmic marketing, by contrast, is very loving, very trusting, very heart oriented. It is not about desperation; it is about expectation. You expect that your vibes are going to go up right now: you're going to feel better right now, which is worth its weight in gold all by itself. Then on a metaphysical level, you're going to be receiving returns in unexpected ways down the road. Knowing that takes away the desperation. Karmic marketing emphasizes the

giving, whereas conventional forms of marketing emphasize the getting.

When you come from karmic marketing, you've
already won. You've already gotten the benefit. Yes, I
expect there to be a material reward ten times over down
the road, but in this moment, the act of giving is its own
reward.

Principle number four: karmic marketing gives freely
from the heart, wanting to share and help, and not expecting anything in return from those you are giving to. Most
forms of marketing, selling, and advertising are focused
on the get: What am I getting out of this? Is my ad, my
news release, my website, my email going to get me sales?

I'm talking about a complete paradigm shift, which
goes back to beliefs and the fact that we are living in an
optical illusion. If we take on this new way of marketing,
we're already complete, we're already satisfied, and our
focus is on giving. On some level, we know that our giving
is going to make a difference, and it's going to come back;
we just don't know how.

I'm not asking people to replace conventional marketing with karmic marketing. I'm not urging you to drop
everything you're already doing. I'm saying add karmic
marketing to what you're doing. That's going to make the
difference.

Andres Pira, with his real estate company in Thailand, is still doing all the traditional forms of advertising

and marketing, but he's added karmic marketing. When he did, his business took off.

Terry Jones has probably been giving throughout his life. But when I asked him about why he gave two Nexersys systems to me, he said that it really began about twenty years ago. He was with a partner who had disappointed him; they broke up, and that business ended. Terry started his new business with a different attitude, which included giving when it felt good to give. He was using karmic marketing, although he didn't know the term. As he did, his business improved. Nexersys is being picked up by big gyms around the world.

Principle five builds upon some things I've already discussed: karmic marketing is built on a foundation of trust, giving, and being detached from outcomes, whereas traditional, desperate forms of marketing are built on distrust and being attached to outcomes.

Again, we're looking at mindset—what people are believing either consciously or unconsciously on all those different levels. If they believe that business is risky, if they believe they don't deserve success, if they believe business is competitive, a dog-eat-dog world, if they believe that marketing is slimy, if they have any of these negative beliefs, their feeling of desperation will probably be at the forefront, leading the way for them.

Karmic marketing is a completely different way of looking at life. Years ago, I wrote a book called *Faith*, in which I said there were three kinds of faith: faith in yourself, faith in other people, and faith in the world—the world meaning God, cosmos, nature, Gaia, whatever you want to call the power that animates all of life, including you and me.

Most people don't have faith, although they say they do: "I have faith that this is going to work. I have faith in myself. I have faith in my family, friends, my partners, my vendors. I believe they're going to do what they're going to do." But they don't really believe it. Underneath is the idea, "They might rip me off. They may not actually do what they said they're going to do. I might not be able to fulfill what I've promised. My customers may drop the ball. The world may not actually be a benevolent place. Maybe it's a scary, threatening place." All of those beliefs can undermine our success.

Karmic marketing is really about awakening, a new way of being. The old-school way of doing business had a desperate, cutthroat approach, using clever and manipulative marketing. These approaches are all there as choices even today. But I'm pointing to sharing from your heart for a product or service you believe in. If you have one you don't believe in, get out of that business. Find what you do believe in. Find what you are excited about. Then you will naturally exude an organic style of marketing that people will relate to, and you will feel good about it. The desperation will be gone. As you are giving now, you will feel an immediate benefit, you will feel better right now, but you will also shortly benefit in some unexpected way.

When I was thinking about this book, I did a little research, because I wondered, "Is there anything out there on karmic marketing? Did anybody else ever talk about it?" No, but there is a book called *Karmic Management*. Here's the essence of it. If you want to be successful in your business, quit focusing on it. Focus instead on making everybody attached to your business successful. If you have employees, find out what they want in their lives. Find out what would make them successful. You have vendors; find out their dreams, their goals, their intentions. What would make them really successful? The book *Karmic Management* says that the more you focus on other people, the more your business will automatically, naturally, and organically blossom and become prosperous. It's all about getting out of your ego and getting into the well-being of everybody else.

This is the tipping point. This is the new wave of marketing. Forget the old school. Forget the desperation. Come from faith. Come from giving. Come from vibration. Do karmic marketing. Do karmic management. Then expect miracles.

Principle six: karmic marketing operates on two levels: the seen and the unseen. On the level of the seen, it strengthens your relationship with the other person, and on the unseen level, it starts a spiritual circulation.

Let me illustrate this principle with a story. Back in the late 1990s, the Internet was coming to widespread public attention. I was on it as a pioneer, making a name for myself as one of the first online marketers.

I was also looking around to see what other people were doing. There was a fellow by the name of Mike Dooley, who had an email that he would send out every day, containing what he called "thoughts from the universe" on his website tut.com (Think Unique Thoughts).

I would get those thoughts every morning, and it really felt as if the universe was writing to me. I felt good; I felt loved; I felt reminded. This came at a time when I was starting to achieve a little bit of success, but it was before the big waves hit. As I was learning karmic marketing, I thought, "OK, where do I want to give right now?"

I thought about Mike Dooley, so I took a deep breath and wrote a check for $1,000 to him. This was a huge amount of money. I was still coming out of poverty; I was still struggling. I was starting to do a little bit better, but I was not that well off. I didn't really have $1,000 at that time.

Nevertheless, I wrote a check for $1,000 and sent it to Mike Dooley. I was saying thank you. I was expressing appreciation to somebody I did not know and thought I would never meet.

Mike got the check and cashed it. He wrote me a little note and thanked me for it. As years went on, we both became members of the Transformational Leadership Council, a group of self-help teachers, authors, and speakers. We get together a couple times a year for R&R, sharing stories, insights, and experiences.

Mike and I really hit it off. He told me that when he got that check for $1,000, he was at a turning point. He was about to quit sending out those emails, even though he thought they were so important to the world and to himself. He knew that they were inspiring people, but he wasn't getting enough monetary return to keep it going. He was going through a dark night: "Should I just stop this? It's taking up my time and energy, and I've got to pay for the service to send these emails out." Although his list was growing, he didn't really see the result.

At that point, my check arrived. After Mike got it at the post office, he said he almost drove off the road as he was going back to his apartment. He and his brother were trying to start a T-shirt business, and it was struggling. The $1,000 got him through.

I found all this out later. Usually when you do karmic marketing, you don't hear the whole story, but in this case I did. Years later, Mike was invited to be in the movie *The Secret*. He never understood why. He didn't have a best-selling book out at the time. He wasn't really on the radar as a law of attraction practitioner. But Rhonda Byrne, the producer, invited him to be in it.

Mike attributes his movie appearance to me. I don't know why, because I don't remember mentioning him to Rhonda. In any case, to thank me, he sent me a card with his note: "Thank you for everything. Great friendship. Thanks for having me in the move *The Secret*." I thought this was great, and I put the card aside.

A couple of weeks went by, and Mike wrote me, asking if I got his note. I said I did. He wrote back, asking, "Did you get everything in my note?"

I wrote back and said, "Yeah, you wrote a handwritten note."

He wrote back again, asking, "Did you see what I had sent you?"

Fortunately, I had kept the card. I turned it over and, stuck to the back, folded over precisely so that it was hidden by the card itself, was a check. I unfolded it. It was for $10,000: ten times what I had given Mike.

Again, when you practice karmic marketing, you usually don't hear the complete story. But the cosmos wanted me to know what happened. Mike Dooley is a dear friend now and is doing fantastically. He has best-selling books and may still be traveling around the world, inspiring people.

At that point, Mike needed $1,000. I didn't know that, so I didn't send it because of need. I sent it as a thank you. I sent it to practice karmic marketing. In this particular case, $10,000 in cash came from the person I'd given it to.

Let me emphasize why karmic marketing works right now, instantly. As we saw with Terry Jones and Andres Pira, when you initiate karmic marketing, your reward is in the moment. You've already gotten the reward of the feeling. You've already changed your chemistry and your psychology, you've upped your vibration, and you've initiated the spin of the karmic wheel, so that down the road there will be an unexpected payoff ten times over. But you've already gotten the payoff in the moment of giving.

When I wrote the check for $1,000, it was a big gulp for me, but I felt great. There were $1,000 of good feelings in that moment. Yes, I waited for a financial payoff that, in this particular case, happened to come from the same source. But the payoff is different every time. Sometimes there's an immediate return. Sometimes it's the same afternoon. If we're focused on the return, we're missing the point of karmic marketing. Karmic marketing is like karmic giving. We're giving knowing that karma is going to roll back around and reward us. But when we realize that we've already gotten the reward, everything else is gravy.

I wrote a book called *The Miracle*, in which I say there are two kinds of miracles. One is where you're longing for something. When it finally shows up, you exclaim, "Oh, it was a miracle!"

But there's also another miracle. It's the miracle of right now. This moment is all there is. When we practice karmic marketing, if we have an eye on the payday, we might be uncomfortable, because we're always calculating. In our brain we've got an invisible accountant that's saying, "You just gave $1,000; where's your $10,000? Come on, universe. Give it to me now." But if you realize that you've already gotten the payoff and that the other payoff is going to come, you can just go on with your life and keep practicing karmic marketing. You'll get into the ebb and flow of money circulation.

In my book *Money Loves Speed*, I say, "Money has to circulate." As you practice karmic marketing, you're putting money into circulation. When it circulates, sooner or later it comes back to you, because you are in that circulation. In any case, karmic marketing is its own reward, and the payoff is instantaneous.

Principle seven: karmic marketing isn't most effective when it relies on what the market wants; it is most effective when it is infused with what the practitioner loves or is passionate about. College courses on marketing focus on what the market wants and on reading the market. Advertisers do focus groups in order to read trends.

Those methods are deceptive, unreliable, and distracting. When you do a focus group, you're asking people what they may or may not do in regard to a product or service. The truth of the matter is, they don't know. There's a famous quote from Henry Ford: "If I asked the customers what kind of car they wanted, they would have said a horse."

At that time, all that consumers understood was the horse and buggy. The car was so new and so foreign to them that they wouldn't relate to it. The focus group would have said, "This is ridiculous. We can't afford it. There are no roads for it. Where will we get the gas? I'm going to stick with my horse. I just have to feed and water it."

Traditional marketing can be misleading. I recently sold my house in Wimberly, Texas, which I had for twenty-seven years. I gave it to a real estate agent who promised to sell it. I was expecting some pretty great marketing, because she knows me as well as some of my marketing books and materials. But to my disappointment, all she did was list it and sit back and wait. When it didn't sell immediately, she started to say, "The market must think that the price is too high. If we keep lowering the price, sooner or later we'll sell it."

I thought, "Wow. Obviously if you keep lowering the price, you'll sell the house. You can lower the price to $50, and somebody's going to buy it."

If you're selling on price alone, you are putting it on a very weak point. Price is not the only thing to change. You can change the description. You can change the marketing. But the agent was giving the power away to what she called the market.

I heard her say this for a while, and then I thought, "I'm not really a real estate agent, but let me do what I know to do." I wrote a sales letter for my own house. I titled it, "The House of Prosperity." I told about my journey of living in that house for twenty years. Within its walls, I wrote *The Attractor Factor* and *Hypnotic Writing* and came up with programs like *The Fourth Dimension Process*.

I did many things in that house, but I wrote the letter to position the house as the hero. It was almost as if it didn't matter who lived in it; it was the house that mattered. On one level, that is correct, because I built it up. I put in my own gym, studio, office, library, and a walking trail out in the woods. I did many things to make it a prosperous place that would influence my creativity.

I sent out that letter to my list, and, yes, we did get nibbles, and yes, we did sell the house.

She was just the listing agent. She didn't do any real marketing or selling. She gave her power away by saying, "It's the market. The market is doing such and such."

In my mind, I thought, "You're playing victim here, and you're giving all the power away to something you're calling the market." That's what I think is misleading about some of the traditional ways of trying to appease or sell to the market.

To sum up, what's most important in karmic marketing is your passion, your enthusiasm, and your creativity, rather than trying to read the tea leaves and scheme about how people are going to respond. People respond to your heart. If you come from your heart, you sincerely believe in your product or service, and you're demonstrating that integrity, people will feel it, and the right people will respond. That's when the sales can start coming in a simpler, more natural way.

3
Masters of the Art

'Ve been inspired by many of the legends of karmic marketing. Most people don't know the truth about some of these famous figures.

I've already mentioned P. T. Barnum. People associate him with the saying, "There's a sucker born every minute." He did not say that. A competitor said it, and the public attributed it to Barnum. Because Barnum thought any publicity was good publicity for him, he didn't correct this misimpression.

Actually, P.T. Barnum was both a very spiritual and very practical man. The people closest to him called him Reverend Barnum. He had a faith in people, in himself, and in the world that most people don't understand or relate to.

As I said earlier, karmic marketing is really based on faith. Barnum had faith. He also practiced giving. He used the term "profitable philanthropy." In his mind, his giving had a little a calculation to it. Strictly speaking, that's different from karmic marketing, because karmic giving should be without calculation. When Barnum gave, he wanted to know that it was going to come back in a very direct way sometime soon.

For example, there was a famous buffalo hunt that was held in New Jersey in the 1800s. It was very newsworthy, and the press covered it. It was great fun for everybody. The hunt was free. It was well publicized and well attended. Ferries were used to get people to the event. There were stands where people could buy food and drink. People went out and had a great time.

At first, nobody knew who actually put on the hunt. Shortly afterwards, Barnum let it be known that he had put it together. He was the one who marketed it. How did he profit from it? He was the one who leased the boats and leased the stands for the food and drink. Everything people bought for this free event profited Barnum.

As I was reading these stories, I kept thinking, "Barnum understood karmic marketing, although not completely in the way that I'm teaching and practicing it today."

This was in the nineteenth century. People thought differently. The Civil War had ended only recently. It was a time before radio, before television, when phones were just coming into being. We need to take all these things into context.

There were other figures, such as J. C. Penney, who founded the Penney's chain. At the turn of the twentieth century, they were called The Golden Rule stores. These stores were practicing a type of karmic giving in the sense that Penney was good to customers and to his own people. His was one of the first companies that enabled employees to share in profits. Penney also got rid of credit, because he knew that it was bankrupting individuals. The stores were cash only, but Penney brought down the price of the clothing he sold so that people could afford them without going into debt.

Penney was a very spiritual man. He contributed to causes he believed in. He created institutions to help people.

Then we can't forget Bruce Barton. He is not well known today, but back in the 1920s his name was a household word. He was a businessman, congressman, and a best-selling author. He was nominated for president. He was one of the founders of the largest ad agency of its time, BBDO (Batten, Barton, Durstine, & Osborn). Barton wrote many books, including works on sales and marketing. One of his greatest secrets was sincerity. He exuded sincerity and care for other people.

I'll also mention Napoleon Hill. I was recently filmed for a movie about him, specifically his classic book *Think and Grow Rich*. His unfinished autobiography was published recently; it's called *Master Mind*. He had started his memoirs twice, and he didn't finish either set. But editors today pieced them together, eliminated the overlap, and turned them into one readable book.

As I was reading Hill's biography, I thought, "He's practicing karmic marketing." He asked for $100 when he spoke for an evening, which was a lot of money for that period, in the 1920s. In one case, he knew that the community he was speaking to was suffering, so he said, "I'll speak to you for free. I'll waive the $100." He didn't think of gain.

Everybody loved Napoleon Hill's presentation. Unbeknownst to him, the person who had booked him told the attendees, "Napoleon Hill waived his fee. But he has a magazine, and you can all subscribe to it." Hill had waived his fee for $100 out of the goodness of his heart, but he received $6,000 in magazine subscriptions.

If we turn to modern-day examples of karmic marketing, it's more complicated, because many companies are giving as a strategy. They have learned that people want to deal with businesses who are making a difference. They know you're going to make money from them, and they want to know that you're making a difference in the world with that money. Consequently, many companies are giving as a strategic maneuver. That's not what I'm talking about with karmic marketing, which is more of an innocent giving, trusting that the return is going to come.

Having said that, we must give a nod to one of the greatest givers of all time: Andrew Carnegie. In the early 1900s, he wrote a little essay called *The Gospel of Wealth*, in which he said that it was the duty of successful people to give away their fortunes. Don't die with your money, he said, because then you will have failed. Thanks to him, we have about 3,000 libraries around the world, which cost him around $55 million; in present-day dollars, that would probably amount to billions.

More recently, Kraft Heinz has committed the equivalent of $12 million to feed communities affected by the coronavirus. Microsoft gives $25 per hour for any employee doing volunteer work to the charity of the volunteer's choice. Penguin Random House pays $1,200 per employee to help with student loans, which I think is a great thing to do. Exxon has a matching gifts program for employee donations. Coca-Cola has donated $820 million to community sustainability since 1984. They've supported over 300 organizations worldwide. The Disney Corporation has donated over $333 million to nonprofits since 2015. Starbucks has given $6.9 million to nonprofits over the same period. There are books thousands of pages long that list companies and individuals who give. But in almost every case, they're giving in this Barnumlike strategic philanthropy way. It is a smart marketing maneuver, but it's not karmic marketing.

Karmic marketing is giving without the calculation of expectation. The idea of giving for expectation goes all the way back to the ancient Stoics. In the first century AD, the Roman author Seneca the Younger wrote a book called *On Benefits*. But here too the giving is calculated in terms of the benefits you get when you give. For example, it will elevate your status if you're a politician.

I'm trying to bring more of a spiritual awareness to the philosophy of giving: knowing that when you give, you already get the benefit and that in the future there will be a return, although not necessarily in the way you expect or maybe even wanted it.

Principles of Karmic Marketing Masters

1. Get out of your ego and get into the egos of others.
2. Think in terms of stories.
3. Use dialogue to bring your writing to life.
4. Be visual.
5. You are the scriptwriter for your audience's dreams.
6. Remind people of their pain.
7. Make things seem new and even somewhat confusing.

I've discovered some basic principles in the practices of karmic marketing masters. The first is to get out of your ego and get into the egos of others. Don't try to change their mindset. This is the essence of a book I wrote called *Hypnotic Writing*, which came out of my experience as a copywriter.

Far too many people in business are focused on their product, their service, their own selfish indulgence in their offerings. They're forgetting that nobody cares. Everybody wants to know what's in it for them. Whether you're selling a shoe or a shoehorn, you need to be thinking, what do people get as the end result for themselves? Yes, we know you want a profit. Yes, we know you want to make the sale. Why should the other person buy? What's in it for them?

Billionaire Andres Pira is focused on what his customers get, not on what he's going to get. He knows he's going to get something out of it if he helps other people. As one of our famous heroes in self-development, the late Zig Ziglar, kept saying, you can have whatever you want as long as you help other people get what they want. Get out of your ego. Get into their egos. Please them.

Second, people think in terms of stories. We are storied beings. We make sense of the world through our stories. When you answer questions with stories, the answers will stay longer. Stories more entertaining, more educational, and more memorable. They go into our subconscious mind; they can deliver a message that is not filtered out by the conscious mind. People think in terms of stories. We tell stories to one another all the time. They are how we communicate.

I loved P. T. Barnum's autobiography and read it two or three times, partly because he was a great storyteller. He told story after story. They were funny and educational and illustrated key points.

You want to be thinking about stories of people who have benefited from your product or service. As a copywriter, I know one of the easiest ways to write a great sales letter is to let your customer write it. Have somebody give you a testimonial, transcribe it, and say, "I could brag about my product, but here's what Jane Smith says." Then run her testimonial. It's coming from an actual satisfied customer, which will be more believable than if you just said, "My product is great, and here's why."

Principle number three is, think in terms of dialogue to bring the writing to life. If you think of some of the great literature you've read, most likely the most inviting have been the novels and stories that were rich with dialogue. Our eyes go to dialogue on a printed page because it implies personality and immediacy: somebody is speaking right now. We prefer that over reading long descriptions that say so-and-so met so-and-so and said such-and-such.

When I was writing copy, I would have a headline that was an excerpt from dialogue. I knew if it had quotation marks around it, I would increase the readership by 15 percent.

Number four: be visual. Get people to see photos, pictures in their minds.

I've been a hypnotist since the 1960s. As time went on, I became certified as a hypnotist and created my own company called Hypnotic Marketing, Inc. As time went on, I wrote *Hypnotic Writing*, *Advanced Hypnotic Writing*, and *Buying Trances*. The concept of hypnosis is very close to my heart. It's very much a skill that I use.

One thing that makes hypnosis work is the understanding that our minds think in terms of pictures, photos, and images. When we're writing marketing copy, we want to do is paint a picture that people can see in their minds. You want them to be able to visualize it.

That's why one of the most common used words in copywriting is the word *imagine*: imagine what your life will be like when you use my product. You are trying to lead people to visualize their relationship with something they don't have yet.

In hypnosis, we speak of the *waking trance*. Think of a time when you were driving down the road and missed your exit. You went into what's called *highway hypnosis*. Obviously, your eyes were open, but your mind was diverted. Part of you was keeping you a safe driver, but another part of you was entrained by your thoughts. You were in a waking trance.

People also have waking trances when they're so absorbed in a good novel that they don't hear the phone ring or they don't hear something happen in the front of the house. This is, again, because the brain thinks in terms of images, photos, and pictures.

With your clever use of words, you can have the same effect on people. If your writing is rich with sensory detail and you lead them into imagining what they could experience with your product, they will begin to feel it's real. They'll begin to imagine owning it.

Number five is related: you are the scriptwriter for your audience's dreams. Paint the picture of the end result that people will have when they buy your product or service. In his book *Breakthrough Advertising*, the famous copywriter, Eugene Schwartz said that you are the scriptwriter for your client's dreams.

The more I thought about it, I understood where he was coming from. When you do marketing, you want people to imagine their life with the product. They have problems. Hopefully your product or service resolves one of those problems, and you focus on their life with it resolved. Describe what their life is like after they've bought your product or service.

Number six is the converse: remind people of their pain without your product or service: "Oh, you have sore feet? Well, I have comfortable shoes for you." Some swear by this tactic. It's often used in traditional marketing, but it's not my favorite; I think it's rather negative.

I prefer a heart-directed way of doing business: focus on your customers' dreams, on what they really want. I want to focus on the ideal. I know that these people are going through pain because they have a dream. They want life to be a certain way. If I can describe it in the way they are longing for, I will increase the odds that they will want to buy.

I think it's a matter of respect for people, for the fact that these people are just like you and me. I'm thinking of Jimmy Stewart making his famous speech in the movie *It's a Wonderful Life*, where he's telling the greedy banker, "These are the people who live and die in this city. These are the people who are supporting what we do. These are the people who have family and friends and kids."

I feel like giving the same kind of speech: "Look, these people are already hurting. You don't need to remind them of their pain. Remind them of their dreams. If you can fulfill their dreams with your product or service, you will have a connection, and you will make money from it. You'll feel good about it, and so will they."

Let's go on finally to the next principle: the importance of making things new and even somewhat confusing. If something seems very simple and obvious, it's not as hypnotic and doesn't attract people as much.

A few years ago, I had a private songwriting workshop with Melissa Etheridge. I've been a fan of hers for well over twenty years; I was actually a member of her fan club. To be in her home, in her studio, being tutored by her on songwriting, was incredible.

She was absolutely wonderful.

Melissa advised that when you write songs, make people reach a little. Making people slightly confused makes them more intrigued. They lean forward, and they want to know more. If she writes a song, and you don't quite know what it's about on first listening, you're going to listen to it two or three more times, especially if all the other elements—the melody and so forth—are there. (Of course, it's Melissa singing, so you're always going to listen to it more than once.)

This advice is comparable to what we do with karmic marketing. Actually, look at the phrase *karmic marketing*. I could have come up with a more obvious title that communicated what it meant, but I called it *karmic marketing*. Why? For the same reason I called a book years ago *Spiritual Marketing*. I thought it would confuse and intrigue people. I thought it would make them curious enough to ask, "What in the world is karmic marketing?"

Curiosity is one of the most powerful tools at a marketer's disposal. When something is a little intriguing and a little confusing, more people are going to be interested.

The same is true with the word *new*. Anything that's new always brings our attention. This is why the newspapers are always focused on, "What's new? What's different?" We want to know what's new, what's different. There's a built-in trigger in our brain that makes us want to know more. Whether you're writing a song or writing an ad, you want it to be new, different, and maybe slightly confusing.

Let me close this chapter with some of the books that have most influenced me. Robert Collier (1885–1950) was a metaphysical writer. He wrote *The Secret of the Ages*, *The Secrets of the Mystic Masters of the Far East*, and *Prayer Works*. These were among the New Agey books that were comforting and mind stretching to me as I was growing up.

Only decades later did I discover that Collier was actually a copywriter—one of the greatest direct mail writers of all time—and he wrote a book called *The Robert Collier Letter Book*. It's a huge manual on how to write sales letters. He includes actual letters that he had written and used, and he tells phenomenal stories about the results that they got.

Again, Collier didn't speak of karmic marketing as such, but one common principle in direct mail is giving a sample of your product or service. He talks a lot about writing sales letters that begin the process of making the sale by giving a little of what you want people to buy.

John Caples is a legendary copywriter. In 1925, he wrote one of the most famous ads in history: "They laughed when I sat down at the piano. But when I began to play..." It was in quotes, like dialogue. Caples was a genius, and he wrote several books about how to write copy, including *Making Ads Pay.* I would definitely read John Caples if you want to do anything with marketing.

I've also mentioned *Karmic Management.* It's like a companion to this material in this book. *Karmic Management* is by three different authors, two of whom are Buddhist monks. As I've already pointed out, its message is that you will be more successful in your business if you focus on helping everybody related to it to be more successful. In fact, they say, "Have zero focus on your own success and 100 percent focus on the success of the people that are touching your business." This include customers, vendors, suppliers—anybody that you deal with. *Karmic Management* says, "Do that, and you will have phenomenal success."

4

Reasons We Don't Give

E ven after I've introduced many of the core principles
of karmic marketing, some people may not be con-
vinced that they are practical enough to produce results.
Some may grant that karmic marketing is a more humane
or spiritual approach to marketing, but they may think,
"At the end of the day, the world is a tough and competitive place. Sometimes I'm going to need to play by tough
rules to feed my family and put a roof over my head."

When I was still stumbling around with the idea of
giving, I too was very skeptical. I thought, "Does this
giving really work? Is that what made Andrew Carnegie

famous? Is that what made John D. Rockefeller wealthy?" Like many people, I was afraid that if I gave money, it might not come back, or that I was being suckered by a principle that didn't serve anybody but the people who were telling me to give. I was so much in fear that it felt difficult to give $1, let alone $5.

I decided I was going to experiment with this principle. I kept a record of what I was doing and turned it into a little book called *The Greatest Money-Making Secret in History,* because I thought, "Who would be able to resist a title like that?"

The greatest money-making secret in history is giving money. So why don't we do it? Why did I not do it? It was because of beliefs. Beliefs about money. About deserving. About trust. About faith. About life in general.

I knew Andrew Carnegie gave. I knew John D. Rockefeller gave. I knew some of the greatest tycoons were giving, and they attributed their success to it.

When I started to give, I did so reluctantly. At the time, I was inspired by an author named Barry Neil Kaufman, who helped create the option method, which is a way of questioning beliefs. It helped teach me to investigate beliefs in order to release them.

I wanted to practice this great money-making secret. I wanted to give some money, and I thought of Barry Neil Kaufman. Then I thought about how little I had. I wrote a check for $5, and I sent it to him.

Later I got to meet Barry. He was one of the most charismatic orators of all time; he was hypnotic in his speaking. He mentioned how I gave $5 and how it made a difference to him as an acknowledgment of his work.

Now I was a little embarrassed because I thought, "$5? That's not very much money." But it was beginning to open the window that I referred to earlier. It began to open me up to the idea that the more I gave, maybe the more I could receive.

Even after I had sent that $5 check, I was still skeptical and scared. I tried the idea of giving on something else. I said, "If this principle of giving really works, what if I gave books?" That seemed easier, partly because I was a book reviewer at the time, and publishers and authors were sending me books free in the hopes that I would review them.

I decided I would start giving away books. If somebody sent me an astrology book, I would find somebody interested in astrology and give it to them. If I was sent a marketing book, I would find somebody interested in marketing and give it to them. I found that the more I gave books, the more books came to me.

It started to dawn on me that this principle works in every area. If you want love, start giving love. If you want attention, start paying attention. If you want books, start giving books. If you want more money, give more money.

I also realized that there are three basic types of giving. The first is *tithing*. Most people have heard of tithing, probably in a religious context. The idea is to give 10 percent of your income to your church, your minister, or your religious cause. There's a long history of tithing, going back to the Old Testament, and it is still practiced today.

I've understood tithing as giving this 10 percent as a kind of a payment for what you have already received. Strictly speaking, it's not karmic marketing, because tithing isn't giving to receive more; it's to pay for what you've already received.

The second form of giving is *seeds*. In 1960 a little book came out called *Seed Money*, by John Speller. It was later reprinted under the title *Seed Money in Action*.

Seed Money discusses the free-will offering of money, knowing you are planting seeds—money seeds—that will bear fruit later. You give seed money to whatever has inspired you. It could be an Uber driver, a waiter, an author, a police person. You ask yourself who or what inspired you in the last week, and you give money to that person, place, or thing. Seed money can attract ten times what you've given. *Seed Money in Action* has countless stories and biblical references proving that it works.

The third is *alms*. Alms is giving, generally in secret, to the poor. This could be the homeless or causes to end poverty. Many people like to parade their almsgiving, even on social media, but it is much more powerful when you do it in secret.

Of these three types, seed money is the closest to karmic marketing. It's a free-will offering to a spiritual source in the knowledge that you are planting seeds with money. It's going to come back to you with money down the road.

You can make mistakes in your giving. I mentioned one earlier, because I was doing it too: it's giving too little. Why do we give too little? Because we believe there isn't enough.

As I've said, I want this book to awaken people. It's more than karmic marketing; it's an expansion of our consciousness. We want to leave scarcity, lack, and limitation behind, and we want to move into abundance, success, benevolence. Both are available to us because of the nature of the universe we live in, but we can choose to see the richer version.

When many people tithe, they give less than 10 percent. They'll ask, "Is this after taxes?" Questions like this are to avoid paying the full amount. They're coming out of scarcity consciousness. Even when it comes to seed money, they'll think, "Let me just give a buck, and let me see if I get $10 back." They give in a skeptical, desperate way. They're not experiencing abundance, because they don't feel abundance.

The people that brag about almsgiving are violating the rule that says it's supposed to be done in secret. If you're broadcasting it or boasting about it, you're coming from your ego, not from a pure heart.

In any event, the number one thing people do wrong is giving too little. I definitely understand this impulse, because I've been there. Nevertheless, I'm challenging you right now to give an amount that makes you feel uncomfortable. It will expand your wealth consciousness. It will expand the set point of your receiving.

Inside of us, on a subconscious level, we have a comfort zone, and we like to play within that zone. But when we stretch it, we can have, do, and be more. I'm inviting you to give seed money to your most recent source of spiritual nourishment. Make the amount a little uncomfortable.

I'm not saying go into debt; I'm not saying break the bank; I'm not saying borrow money. Just make it a little uncomfortable. How much would you give if you believed this method might actually work? Give that amount. As you do, pay attention to your thinking, because the thoughts that come up will be related to your giving, and they need to be looked at. I will talk about clearing beliefs in chapter 5, but let's begin right now. I challenge you to give a little bit more than you're comfortable with to your most recent source of spiritual inspiration.

It's a continual process. As you get comfortable with that amount, stretch it even more. Keep working on the outer edges of that comfort zone in your giving. We want to keep stretching. We want to keep growing. Keep doing

a little more till you're at the point where you can be giving thousands, tens of thousands, hundreds of thousands,
knowing that if you're giving that much money, you must
have that much or more available to you.

Play with the dream. Again, we're the scriptwriters of
our own dreams. Play with the dream of being so secure
in your faith in your wealth that it almost doesn't matter
how much you give: you know you're getting ten times
more. You also know that the payoff is right now, because
you've elevated your wealth set point to a vibrational level
that gives you goosebumps all over, because it's so deli-
cious. That feeling is the immediate payoff, and it attracts
even more abundance.

This approach seems to fly in the face of many popular money management experts. They often advocate a
more miserly strategy: pay everything off, and build up
huge amounts of reserves. They are illustrating the two
optical illusion choices that I've been talking about. They
are speaking to the people who are living in scarcity, who
believe in lack and limitation. It's good that these experts
are addressing this audience, because those living in the
mentality of scarcity, lack, and limitation need that kind
of help. They need somebody to say, "Here's what you do
with your money. Here's how to protect yourself. Here's
how to stay in survival."

I'm talking about the other way of living—about
living in a benevolent universe, in a place of peace and

prosperity. I'm talking about listening to people like Bill Gates and Warren Buffett. These guys created the Giving Pledge way back in 2010. They are extraordinarily wealthy people who have committed themselves to giving the greatest part of their wealth away. The Giving Pledge has 211 members the last time I checked. The late Percy Ross is another multimillionaire who spent his life giving away his earnings. These are the people that inspire me.

This is the kind of mentality we want to have: as we give, we will grow and prosper. And as we do, we can give even more.

Those who are struggling to hold on to what they have are stuck in a mindset according to which they need help to survive. At some point, I hope they will awaken and live from a prosperity consciousness. In this consciousness, giving is easier, receiving is faster, and it makes a difference on all levels. The miracle of the future and the miracle of this moment all take place. It's a very natural, organic process, free from desperation.

There are some blocks that prevent people from receiving what's justly due to them. Most people have difficulty doing and receiving good things for themselves, because on some deep level they don't feel worthy. They don't feel lovable. They don't feel good enough. This could make it difficult for them to receive money, even though they're practicing karmic marketing.

A backdoor way of elevating your own level of success is to help other people. Let me explain. My guitar teacher and coproducer Guitar Monk Mathew Dixon came up with an idea a while back called "attracting for others," and he wrote a little book called *Attracting for Others*. It's free. You can go to attractingforothers.com and download it.

According to this concept, when you hear that somebody wants something, when somebody mentions that they have a goal or are struggling with a problem, you imagine they achieve, attract, and accomplish whatever they're seeking. You don't have to express this wish. You don't have to verbally tell them or do anything in actuality (unless there is something that you can do for them).

This is more of an internal approach to success. Why is it important? Most people will find it easier to help somebody else than themselves. If at lunch I overhear Betty the waitress say she wants to open up her own coffee shop, in my mind, I will see her opening up her own coffee shop. In my thoughts, I will acknowledge that she has her own coffee shop. I am internally attracting for her. This helps me get a little closer to success and owning it for myself. Until I can raise my own sense of deservingness, I can do it for others. It's a backdoor approach to success.

Help other people. This fits in with the advice in *Karmic Management*, which says, don't focus on yourself at all; focus on the people related to your business. Help them be successful, and you'll be successful. That's karmic management. It's a backdoor approach to succeeding for yourself.

Another way of opening yourself up to abundance is spiritual mind treatment. This a way to correct some of the negative limiting beliefs that could have prevented success, happiness, and wealth in the past.

A spiritual mind treatment is a simple prayerlike process. You don't have to do anything in particular except listen, allow, and receive. You can do it right now.

Pause for a moment, let your breath relax, and say: *I know there is an infinite energy system in the universe that is of me, in me, and around me. We are all connected to it, are in it, and are of it. I am connected to you as well as to everyone else through the energy that sustains us. I know that when I give anything into this energy system, it will return to me in kind, multiplied and amplified, because the nature of the system is to grow and expand. I am grateful for this realization and for the gifts I have now, am receiving, and will receive. I trust the process to work for me as it does for everyone who activates it with giving. So be it. It is so.*

You can return and do that over and over again.

Here's another approach. Ask yourself, *if I thought like God, what would I do right now?* Decades ago, when I lived in Houston and I was beginning as a speaker, I went to a small church. For whatever reason, I was inspired to talk about how God might think. I said, "If you thought like God, what would you be thinking? If you thought like

God, would you have fears? If you thought like God, what would your goals be? What would you go for? How big would you think? If you thought like God, what would you do right now?"

I still touch base with those questions. Sometimes when I'm reflecting on a new project, I'll ask myself, "If I thought like God, would there be any limitations? If I thought like God, would there be any boundaries? Would anything be off-limits? Would there be anything I couldn't create?"

That question frees me, empowers me, and enlarges my confidence in my ability to achieve things at a level that previously I couldn't even imagine.

I invite you to think like that. Whatever your concept of God, the Divine, or a higher power is, if you thought like this being, what would you be thinking? Would you be afraid to give? Would you worry about receiving? Would you in any way, shape, or form drop your faith in yourself, in other people, in the planet?

No. When you think like God, all the excuses, the negative beliefs, the lack and limitations are gone. Would God live in a lack and limitation universe and give in a scared, skimpy way? No. Thinking like God helps us free and empower ourselves.

Receiving is another big issue. People have problems with receiving because it reflects their own level of self-esteem and deservingness.

When I was with my first wife, Marian, both of us were greatly inspired by Leo Buscaglia, Dr. Love, who used to appear on PBS television. He bragged about having the copyright on love.

Dr. Leo was so affectionate, so wonderful. He came to Houston, where we were living at the time, and we waited in line to get a hug from him. It took two hours, because he sat with each person, and he was in no hurry. He was totally present. He looked people right in the eye, he asked about their lives, and he shared. He did the same with us when we got to him.

A little later, Marian wanted to thank him. She decided to send him a gift—seed money—so she wrote a check. Remember, we were struggling. Writing a check for any amount was a big strain for us. But Marian wrote a small check and sent it to Leo Buscaglia.

A week or so later, the check came back. There was a nice note from Leo, but he rejected the check. He said he didn't need it. He had been recently robbed, and he realized that he didn't really need anything. He lived in his empty apartment and was glad to have it, and he suggested she give it to somebody else.

Marian was devastated. Leo had blocked the reception of her love. I thought, "He could have received it. Even if he didn't want it, he could have passed it on to somebody else. He could have given the check to a homeless person. He could have cashed it and given the money away." But he didn't, and it confused me until I got into a similar situation.

I was giving a talk about karmic marketing at a big convention. Afterwards, one of the people at the presentation came up to me: Lori Anderson, who later became a friend of mine; she wrote a book called *Divorce with Grace*.

Lori said, "Joe, I'd like to give you a gift." It was a handmade drum which I knew cost $1,000 and which I really wanted.

When I started thinking about the drum, my hands started to sweat. I felt uncomfortable and embarrassed. I said, "I don't really want you to do that, because that costs $1,000."

"No," she said. "I really want to do it for you. If you would like to have the drum, we will go over and buy it."

I said, "OK." We went over, and she bought the drum. Later I found out that the man who made it was there; he was broke, and he needed money. He needed $1,000 to pay his rent and take care of his bills and groceries.

Lori's gift to me had side benefits that I didn't know were going to happen. But I also realized, "Wow! Receiving is almost harder than giving."

When I looked deeper, I realized that my reluctance had to do with my sense of deserving. I thought, "I don't really deserve this. I didn't really do anything." But Lori wasn't giving it to me because I did anything to deserve it. She was doing it from her heart, from her wanting to share. I think Leo Buscaglia missed that moment by returning the check to my wife.

Money needs to circulate. As we give in karmic marketing, we are entering the flow of circulation. When it comes back around to us, it's still in circulation, but if we don't receive, we block that circulation, making it difficult for us to receive any more gifts. We put up a detour sign. When the cycle is coming back around, we say, "No, don't come here," and we send it somewhere else.

Let me tell you one more story about receiving. A few months ago, I got a phone call. The person on the phone said he had a gift for me; he wanted me to go to the front door, where it would be leaning against the wall. I went to the front door, found a giant box, brought it in, and carefully opened it up. Inside was a beautiful, handmade, collectible, electric V-shaped guitar made by Tony Nobles, one of the most noted luthiers of all time. It was breathtaking. I stared at it and choked up.

When I opened the case and I saw the guitar, I lost my breath, because it was so spectacular. I knew its value. It was handmade, with brass, gold, a whammy bar, and many other details, so I knew it was worth almost $10,000. And it was given to me!

Later, I got a message from the person who had left it, and I figured out who it was. They said they only had one request and that was never to say who gave it to me. They wanted to remain anonymous.

I still felt uncomfortable in receiving, but unlike when Lori gave me the drum, I was far better at it. I think I've stepped into the flow of the circulation of giving and receiving to enable it to do even bigger things.

That's the point of the story. Practice karmic marketing—which is entering the flow of circulation—and as it comes back, open your arms and open your heart. Even if it's a sweaty palms moment, receive, because that continues the circulation.

People sometimes object to karmic marketing on the grounds that giving things away for free doesn't establish any value for people. They argue that people only value something when it costs them something: they reframe that cost as an investment. You see this strategy all over the world, from information to hotel rooms to cars to premium college educations.

Karmic marketing is about giving without caring what the other party decides to do with the gift. Obviously you hope that it will benefit them, but it doesn't really matter. It's like the Bob Proctor quote that I mentioned previously: "If I give money to somebody, and they take it and burn it, it does not matter." He gave out of the purity of giving, because that's what he wanted to give. At the point that it is released from him and goes into the hands of the person receiving it, it's out of his control. It is now under the choice of the recipient. If they want to devalue it, they can. If they want to dismiss it, they can.

If they want to give it away, they can. If they want to sell it, they can.

When Lori gave me the drum, I could have resold it. But I took it because I valued the drum. For the record, I still have that drum and still use it and love it, and I love the memory of Lori giving it to me.

Robert Cialdini, author of *Influence: The Psychology of Persuasion*, one of the greatest of all books on the subject, talks about reciprocity. He says that when you give, you set off a mechanism in people's minds. They start thinking, "This person gave, so I need to give back."

There's a little bit of that going on with karmic marketing, but that's not why you're doing it. You're not giving to a person, place, or thing to get from that person, place, or thing. You are giving because of the feeling you're getting—that's vibrational giving—so you've already got your payoff. You've already got the benefit. What the other person does with it is entirely up to them. It doesn't matter at all. They can do whatever they want. You didn't give to get a particular response from the recipient. You gave knowing you're going to be rewarded down the road in an unexpected way from somebody, who may or may not be the same person. But you're not banking on it being the same person.

5

Eradicating Limiting Beliefs

Karmic marketing always works. There is no exception. When somebody tells me, "I'm practicing karmic marketing, but it doesn't seem to be coming back as much or as rapidly as I want," I immediately know that certain beliefs are in play that block it. When people practicing karmic marketing are waiting for money to come back, if they unconsciously still think it's bad, they'll block it. If it shows up in their lives, they'll quickly get rid of it.

I went through this phase. During my poverty, I was reading all the self-help books and applying their ideas as best I could. I would wonder, "How come it doesn't seem to be working for me? Is there something wrong with me? Is there something wrong with my thinking? Is there something wrong with my genetics? Is there a curse on me?"

As you read this book, you too may be thinking, "The law of attraction works for everybody else, but it doesn't work for me." When I hear that, I know that behind it are beliefs which are inhibiting the results that the person wants.

Limiting Beliefs about Money

1. Money is the root of all evil.
2. There's not enough to go around.
3. If I'm successful, people will hate me.
4. If I have more than I need to get by, someone else has to go without.
5. If I make a lot of money, I will betray my parents.
6. Money is hard to get.
7. You have to sacrifice other values, such as your family, to become wealthy and successful.
8. To save money, you have to do without.
9. Money is not spiritual.
10. I will never have enough.
11. I don't deserve to have a lot of money.

One of the biggest beliefs is one I have encountered in every country I have been to—Russia, Ukraine, Iran, Italy, Poland, Bermuda, Canada, America. It explains why money is such a struggle for so many people. Here's the belief: money is the root of all evil.

This belief is in the culture. It is in the collective unconscious, if you want to use Carl Jung's term, and it operates on a level that we're mostly blind to. We read a book on the law of attraction, goal setting, or even this material on karmic marketing. People give money, and they know to expect it's going to come back down the road. But if you think money is evil, will you actually want it to come back? If you think money is evil, will you actually want to profit in your business? If you think money is evil, are you going to allow it to show up in any big way? This is the primary reason most people struggle with money. I went through this phase, just like everybody else.

I want to unpack this belief and clear it for you right now. Even if we only hit this belief, this is the gold mine. This is the lotto win for everybody.

"Money is the root of all evil" is an incomplete part of a longer statement from the Bible: "The love of money is the root of all evil" (1 Timothy 6:10).

That's only slightly better. Instead of saying money is evil, we're saying the love of money is evil. Let's unpack it. When I look at people who have money and are healthy, happy, and well adjusted, I don't see people who are in love with money. They appreciate money, which leads to one of my favorite quotes of all time. It's from Arnold Patent's book *Money* (another book I recommend). He said, "The sole purpose of money is to express appreciation."

This idea can transform your relationship to money. When you realize that its sole purpose is to express appreciation, you see that it has nothing to do with money being evil. It has nothing to do with being in love with money. You are using it as a tool.

When I first read that quote, I thought, "There has to be an exception to that. The sole purpose of money is to express appreciation? Maybe not."

Then I started thinking. When I pay a bill, I'm grateful to have a phone. When I make a payment for a mortgage, a car, Internet service, or electricity, I'm thinking, "I'm really grateful to have a house; I'm grateful to have utilities." I started to realize that money is my way of saying thank you. I'm saying thank you for these services.

That's not the way I felt for most of my life. I grumbled. I thought, "There isn't enough money. Money is evil. There's a shortage of it, and I'm hurting every time I write a check." Now I'm thinking, "Thank you."

If we look at the situation this way, we demolish the belief that money is the root of all evil.

Let me give another example. I have often held up a pen in front of an audience and said, "Is this pen bad? Is this pen evil?" People will chuckle. I'll go on: "With this pen, I could stab you. I can write an angry letter and upset you. I can create propaganda that moves people to do negative things. Yet with this same pen, I could write a love letter. I could write a great American novel. I could write a script. I can write positive affirmations. I can rescript my life. I can use the pen for what some would call evil or some would call good. Is the pen evil? Is the pen good? The pen is a pen. It's neutral. In and of itself, it is nothing but a writing instrument."

Money is the same. In and of itself, it is nothing but a means of barter. It is innocent. As we strip away all the negativity around money, we can allow it to come to us.

Money is neutral. It's a tool for fulfilling your life mission and your dreams. Walt Disney said, "I want to make money from my movies so I can continue making movies." I love the purity here. He didn't want money because to be the greatest director in film history. He wanted money to continue doing what he loved, which was creating more movies.

Much like me. I want to make money from my books. Why? So I can continue writing more books. I want to make money from my music. Why? So I can continue creating more music. Money is good.

People subconsciously hold on to guilt about money because of the idea that there's not enough to go around: if I have more than I need to get by, someone else has to go without. They feel that if they take so much for themselves, somebody else down the line is getting less.

This comes from the old-school way of looking at the world. In this optical illusion called life, you can look out and see scarcity. You can see lack and limitation, and you can find evidence for it. You can say, "We're losing resources, and if I make money, other people won't."

Yet if you come from the abundance mentality—which is just as real and just as available—you can find the evidence that we are finding new ways of creating and new ways of sharing. People have worried that we will run out of oil, much like in the 1970s, when everybody was standing in line to get gas.

What happened? We've found new ways to create fuel. We're using hybrid automobiles. We're looking at battery-powered cars, which have always been around; in fact, the first car was electric. We are great at adapting, discovering, and finding different materials to get things done. There isn't any limit. Shortage is an illusion. It is a choice. It is not true.

When I was in poverty and homelessness, I would have said, "There are not enough jobs. If there were, I'd have one."

Now that I'm in a different position and have a different mindset, I look out and say, "There's more than enough. Some employers can't find enough people to hire."

There is plenty of money to go around. Trillions of dollars are in circulation right now. They are circulating because people are buying, selling, investing, saving, and giving money so it keeps going around.

There are no real limits in the world, except the ones that we buy into. The only limit is our mind. All the limits are beliefs or mental constructs. Of course, a skeptic can say, "Oh, no, that's not true. Let me give you this example," but the example they will give is itself a belief, a mental construct. If you really whittle it down, you will find that it doesn't hold up to reality.

Another mistaken belief is that if I'm successful, people will hate me. This goes back to the idea that we're in a competition. It's another aspect of the old-school approach to doing business. From this standpoint, I could see some of my best friends as competitors, because we're in the same business, doing the same thing. Yet we are allies. We help one another. Our level of consciousness is such that we see one another as beloved friends who can support each other, not as enemies on opposite sides of some brutal game.

It's not about having other people hate me because I'm successful. I feel that the more successful I become, the more people will be inspired by me. Instead of taking the old, limiting belief, I have adapted a new one.

Another limiting belief: if I have more than I need to get by, someone else has to go without. That's the win-lose scenario. It is not true. After we were finished filming *The Secret*, we looked around at everybody in the room and said, "Does anybody else have any questions?"

A cameraman who hadn't said anything during the filming said, "If we all go for what we want, won't we run out of stuff?"

I said, "Turn the camera back on." That led to one of the greatest moments in the movie *The Secret*, when I said, "There is no way we're going to run out of everything. We don't all go for the same thing. Not everybody wants a Rolls-Royce. Not everybody wants a particular pen. Not everybody wants the same house. Not everybody wants the same anything." The whole idea of win-lose is, again, coming from the old way of looking at the world.

Another limiting belief: if I make a lot of money or I'm very successful, I will betray my parents. I had to wrestle with this one, because early on in the Internet marketing days, I started to make quite a bit of money; then I hit a ceiling. It perplexed me because I thought, "This is the Internet. There's nobody stopping me from making more money. What is going on? There's an invisible barrier."

When I looked more deeply, I realized that I was afraid my father would be embarrassed if I was more successful than him. Then I had to do what I recommend: question that belief. I realized, no, he's not going to be embarrassed; he will be proud.

In fact, as I became more successful, my father became one of my biggest promoters, bragging about me to family, friends, neighbors, and anybody who would listen. This was another belief that didn't hold up to the spotlight of awareness.

Some believe that money is hard to get. Actually, there are many ways to bring in money. Some might seem hard to you, but if you do what you love and joyfully pursue your dream, it may look hard to other people, but it'll be easy for you.

People say to me, "You wrote eighty books? My God, you must never sleep. You must never take a break."

I'm thinking, "Writing books is a joy to me. It would be hard for somebody who doesn't want to do it, but for somebody who does want to do it, it's part of their flow. It's part of their passion."

Another belief: you have to work hard and sacrifice other values, such as your family, to become wealthy and successful. But many people involve their entire families in their work. There's a reality TV show called *Wahlburgers*. It's about a hamburger chain owned by the Wahlberg family. You may know the name Mark Wahlberg. He's one of the most famous young actors of all time, and he's been in sixty-five movies. He's worth $300 million. He and his family run a hamburger business, and they have chains all over the United States, Dubai, and China. The program shows this family working together. They're not sacrificing their family; they're including their family to become wealthy and successful. Of course, this is merely one example; there are plenty of other ways to succeed.

To move on to another belief: to save money, you have to do without. That's not true. It's coming from the either/ or mentality: "If I have one thing, I have to give up something else." Why can't you have both? Again, how would you think if you thought like God? Would God go either/ or? Would God say, "If I get the car, I can't have the bike"? No, God would say you can have both. You can have anything you want.

Yet another belief: money is not spiritual. To me, money is one of the most powerful and spiritual of all forces. It can enable you to fulfill your life mission. It is part of what has been given to us to achieve our goals, to make a difference in the world. If you care about the poor, if you have causes you believe in and you really want to make a difference, money is one of the most powerful tools you can use. From that standpoint, money is spiritual.

Mother Teresa did not put down money; she welcomed it and looked for more. Gandhi and other great leaders and teachers were not focused on money, but they used it for their goals. Money is indeed spiritual.

There are many other such beliefs. One thing you can do right now is listen to your self-talk. What are you telling yourself as you read this? Are you agreeing or arguing? Are you saying, "Yeah, Joe, but what about the idea that money doesn't bring happiness?" Beliefs may be surfacing in your mind that I'm inviting you to criticize, examine, and release. One famous actress said, "If you think money doesn't buy happiness, you don't know where to shop."

The reality is that money just makes things a little bit easier for people. It's not about being happier because you have money; it's about being freer.

I invite you to examine all these beliefs. Again, as you are reading, what beliefs surface? What is your self-talk? That chatter is revealing a limiting belief. Examine it and release it.

Karmic marketing absolutely works. It's like a law of the universe. But you can stop it or slow it down if you retain any limiting beliefs about deservingness, receiving, or money.

There's a belief that comes up in some people who are very wealthy. It's the idea that I will never have enough, that I have to keep earning. It's almost a compulsion.

To explore this issue, let me begin by pointing out that almost everybody thinks money is going to be the solution to all their problems. I thought that during my time of struggle. I run into people who say, "I really want to win the lottery"; they're putting their salvation on a big windfall. These people look at the wealthy and say, "They're well-off. They're living luxurious lives. What's wrong? Why do they think they need to have still more?"

Even though these people are rich, there's a scarcity mindset that's going on inside of them. They're being driven to fill a hole that can't be filled. They need to move into a more spiritual awareness, advance into the miracles of life, and realize that everything in this moment is a miracle. Everything in this moment is satisfactory. Everything in this moment is complete. You may want more down the road, but if you can be in this moment with gratitude, you don't have to struggle or strive, especially when you already have more than enough by most people's standards.

Many years ago, I went to Kuwait. A princess paid to bring me over there. I did not want to go, so I raised my rates and told her I wanted all kind of things. But she gave me everything I wanted, and flew me first-class all the way from Texas to Kuwait.

This princess put on a self-improvement event for people in Kuwait, because she believed that people like me could make a difference over there. She paid to set this up. She paid to get the media there. She paid her speakers, including me, top dollar. She was independently wealthy because she was born in Kuwait. If you are born in Kuwait, you start receiving money from the oil reserves at birth. In addition, she had married twice to two very rich men, and both died and left her their colossal wealth. She had tripled the wealth in her life and was spending money to make a difference for her people.

Afterwards, we sat down and she said, "I'm thinking of hiring you as a coach."

I thought, "What in the world would she need me for?"

"Because I have a problem with money," she said. "I feel guilty that I have all this immense wealth and I have done nothing."

There it was. We were all thinking, "We really want to be like the princess. To be born into a country where

wealth is handed to you, and you are immediately independently wealthy just by birth. And then to go through
this life where more money is given to you over time, and
you really can't spend it all."

She talked about buying cars. She would say, "I'm
interested in a particular car." The dealership would drive
it to her home, and she'd say, "Oh, no, I don't want that
one. I want a different color." They would drive it back, get
another car, and drive it to her. This was the kind of life
she was living. Yet underneath it was a doubt about her
deservingness.

In short, if we believe we have problems with money,
if we believe we don't deserve it, if we believe that we can't
receive good things, if we question the nature of money or
think it's evil, all of this will interrupt the circulation that
makes karmic marketing work.

Yes, karmic marketing is part of it. Yes, giving to your
source of spiritual nourishment is part of it. Yes, expecting tenfold return in some unforeseen way is part of it.
Nevertheless, limiting beliefs need to be cleared. When
you discover a belief of this kind, you want to ask, "Why
do I believe that? Why do I believe that?"

We're looking for evidence from our past. Maybe we
heard it from a family member. Maybe we heard it from
somebody in the media. Maybe we heard it repeatedly
growing up. Maybe it's in the culture. Where did it come
from?

We want to be a kind of loving belief detective, looking for the origin of the belief, trying to find its first cause. As we look for it, we ask, "Is that belief true? Is there evidence for it?"

We want to find out whether this belief is a fact. Is it is factual and scientific, so that everybody would agree on it? Or is it open to interpretation? That would indicate that it is merely a belief, a view, a perception. It's not necessarily reality.

Belief can become reality, but when you question the beliefs, you change the reality. So the second question is, is it true?

The third question would be, "What do I think would happen if I didn't have this belief?" You're looking for the other side of the belief. If you think there isn't enough, you want to question that belief and ask, "What do I think would happen if I did not believe that?"

There'll be an answer, which will be unique to the person asking. It could be, "If I didn't believe in the world of shortage, I'd go out there and I'd spend more money." What would be wrong with that?

Let me give a personal example. When I was growing up, my father said, "The best friend you can have in your life is that dollar bill in your pocket."

I thought, "Wow, this is my dad. This is my authority figure. This is my teacher, my mentor, and I'm a little kid. What do I do with that? I've got to put it in my pocket.

I've got to remember it. I've got to believe that no matter what goes on in my life, I'd better have a dollar bill in my pocket."

My father also said, "If you want to double your money, fold it over and put it back in your pocket."

"That's really clever," I thought. "My dad's really smart. He's wise and he's humorous. What a charming guy. And he learned that the best way to double your money is to fold it over and put it back in your pocket."

As I went through my life and struggled, I wondered, "How come I don't have any money? How come I only have $1? How come I can't seem to bring any money in?"

I was reading books like *Spiritual Economics*, *Think and Grow Rich*, *The Magic of Believing* by Claude Bristol, and other great success literature. They all pointed to beliefs, so I started to ask, "What beliefs might I have?"

Then I heard my father in my head, saying the best way to double your money is to fold it over and put it in your pocket. Now I wanted to ask, "Why do I believe that? Because my dad told me." Is it true? Uh, actually no. You don't double your money by folding it. You still have the same amount of money. But my dad never said that, and I never questioned it until I started to work on belief clearing.

What might I be concerned would happen if I did not have that belief? I might give the money away. I might spend it. I might invest it. What might happen if I did?

Guess what? I would engage karmic marketing, and I would enter the circulation of life. By moving that money out of my pocket and into the world, I would enter the ebb and flow that will bring money back to me.

Anybody can use this process. When you have a belief, you want to look at it, maybe even write it down so you can see it clearly in front of you. Then ask, "Why do I believe it?" Underneath, write any reasons, stories, or memories of where the belief came from. Then ask, "Is it true?" In the light of the fact that you now know where it came from, is this belief true; is it a fact? Could it be open to question? The next question would be, "What are you afraid will happen if you didn't believe it?"

I want to give a bonus question here: what would be a better belief? What belief could you replace the old one with? If you let go of the belief you've been questioning, what could be a more empowering replacement belief?

In an earlier chapter I gave this example: "The more money I spend, the more money I receive." That seemed counterintuitive. It certainly ran counter to my beliefs from my upbringing, but as I made it a new belief, it's now my new reality.

Eliminating negative beliefs clears the runway for takeoff and landing. It clears your path to freely give money, product, service in order to implement karmic marketing and freely receive the tenfold return.

If people implement karmic marketing with the expectation of return and their return seems slow, it's a hint that there are beliefs in the way. As you remove those beliefs, it's like taking the brush off the airport runway, cleaning the path so you can fly off and land. It frees the cycle of circulation to work in your favor. It creates prosperity without any blocks or hitches.

Here are some more books that you can read to reinforce your new beliefs. One is *Spiritual Economics* by the late Eric Butterworth, a Unity minister who had his own radio show. It's about the mindset and spirituality of money and wealth, and it's been out for a long time. It woke me up when I first read it. It helped me dismantle some of the limiting beliefs that I was still carrying. I recommend *Spiritual Economics*: it'll help with some belief clearing.

I would also recommend Napoleon Hill's masterpiece *The Law of Success* as well as his *Think and Grow Rich*, which is a condensed version of *Law of Success*.

Also read my book *Attract Money Now*. It's free: just go to attractmoneynow.com. It offers a seven-step formula for attracting money. The first step is about beliefs.

6
Karmic Marketing in Public Relations

Contrary to popular opinion, the challenge in publishing is not getting published. It's easier to get a book published today than at any other time in history. The challenge of getting published is a wall that most people can climb.

The real wall, which seems insurmountable to most authors, is publicity: making enough people aware that your book is available and worth purchasing. After publishing a book, the work has just begun. The same is true for any product or service.

As I've already mentioned, I discovered that publicity was one of the most underused marketing techniques, although it has been used successfully for centuries. P. T. Barnum used press releases. He befriended the media. He sent out stories to get the newspapers to give him publicity. That free publicity made him and his associates rich and famous.

One of Barnum's greatest success stories was Charlie Stratton, a little boy who would not grow beyond three feet tall. Everybody in Connecticut thought how sad that was. Barnum met Charlie Stratton and saw something other people didn't see. He saw a superstar, and he arranged with Charlie's parents to put him on the circuit, to train him to be a showman. He renamed Charlie "General Tom Thumb." General Tom Thumb became one of the most famous celebrities on the entire planet.

This was, of course, long before anybody knew anything of radio, television, or Internet. It was all done with news releases. Barnum befriended the media. The media loved the story, and they loved General Tom Thumb. They made him rich and famous. That little guy became a multimillionaire and was beloved by virtually everybody. What was the secret? Publicity.

After Barnum's time, Harry Houdini used publicity to make himself the world's first handcuff king, and today we still think of him as the greatest magician of all time. Magicians will tell you that he was not the greatest magician of all time: he was the greatest self-promoter of all time. I say that respectfully, because I am a big fan of Houdini.

So I learned that publicity worked for Barnum, for Houdini, and for all famous people, whether it is Sir Richard Branson, who recently went to the edge of outer space in his own ship, or Elon Musk, who plans to put people on Mars by 2026. These people are creating things to get us to talk about them. How do we know about them? Because publicity is telling the world what they're doing, and we tell each other.

When I come out with a new book, I love to issue a news release talking about what the book is, focusing on the benefit, as well as telling the story behind the book, and I always involve karmic marketing. For example, I came out with a book called *The Miracles Manual*. It's a collection of interviews with me about my Miracles Coaching Program. People in this program have questions about life, death, spirituality, karma, karmic marketing, and everything else. They ask me these questions, and I answer them. We took the best of these and put them in *The Miracles Manual*.

From a karmic marketing standpoint, I thought the wisest thing to do was give this book away. So I put a website up: Miraclesmanual.com. Over time, people started going there and downloading the book. It did so well, I made *The Miracles Manual: Volume 2*, and then *The Miracles Manual: Volume 3*.

In an earlier chapter, I told you about my booklet called *Spiritual Marketing*. When I first wrote it, I implemented karmic marketing even before I had the name, and I gave it away. We estimate that five million people got that book. People are still downloading it even though it's dated, because it's been rewritten and retitled *The Attractor Factor*.

In all these cases, I gave away the books to start the word of mouth and enlist publicity. News releases about *Spiritual Marketing* and *The Miracles Manual* went out so the media could do what it did for Barnum, Houdini, Branson, and Musk. Publicity works because the media wants good stories. Give them good stories, and they will help you.

Many people have a negative image of public relations. Press releases sometimes have a saccharine quality, and as the public reads them, they think, "That company is just trying to put out some generic statement to paper over a problem."

Many businesses boast, saying they're the greatest, but Bruce Barton said that sincerity is one of the lost secrets of success. Now here's something else that's shocking: when I was learning copywriting, one principle that came up is that people will believe you sooner if you admit a weakness. Nobody is perfect. When someone produces a news release that comes across as boasting or bragging—"we're infallible; our product or service does everything; there is nothing it doesn't do"—it doesn't ring true. We know nothing's perfect. We know that in some way, shape, or form, the item or service that you're offering is weak, and you'll hide it because you don't want the public to know.

You want to focus on what's good: that's natural. But the human mind has a little seek and find feature that says, "They're bragging about their product, but there doesn't seem to be anything wrong with it. It must not be real." You've just created a disconnect.

First of all, be sincere. There's something wrong with your product or service. There's something it doesn't do. It's probably OK that it doesn't do it, but if you admit it, this will come across as a sign of weakness, which will give you credibility. People will pick up your sincerity.

Previously I mentioned Andres Pira, the realtor who is now a billionaire in Thailand. I met him a few year ago. When I met him, he had flown me into Bangkok to speak at an event. At the time, he was thirty-five years old. He met me at the airport and told me his story.

Fifteen years before, he was homeless. He was sleeping on the beach in Thailand, which might sound ideal in other circumstances, but he was broke. He had no money, no car, no apartment, no job. He had nothing going for him. He was starving and homeless. He's from Sweden, so he called a friend back home, saying, "I need help."

The friend said, "I'm not going to send you any money, but I'll send you a book." The book was *The Secret*, which was the text version of the movie.

When Andres received the book, he was mad. He started reading it, and thought it was all nonsense. He said, "I'm going to prove this book wrong. I'm going to prove that none of this material works."

Andres started to do everything the book recommends: affirmations, visualizations, meditation. He said, "I want a cup of coffee," and somebody bought him one. He thought, "That's a fluke."

Then Andres started visualizing to attract lunch. Somebody bought him lunch. Now he was starting to think, "Maybe there's something to it." He focused on getting a job and got one. He focused on an apartment and got one.

Fifteen years later, at thirty-five, Andres was a billionaire, the largest real estate developer in southern Thailand. He also has twenty other businesses, including a gym, coffee shops, a firm of attorneys, and more, which he basically runs from his phone.

Andres learned something from Thailand. He said, "In Thailand, the mentality is a gift culture mentality." On people's birthdays, they don't receive gifts; they give gifts. This is karmic marketing at work. On my next birthday, I practiced giving. I said, "I don't want anything on my birthday. I'm just going to give."

Andres Pira built an empire on giving and publicity. He was using publicity to talk about his business. When he opened his first real estate office, he was a nobody with a real estate office who was trying to get attention for himself. Yes, he used the principles in *The Secret*, which is why he brought me to Thailand. He said he owed his success to me, because in that movie I taught him some of the more esoteric practical, psychological principles. But it was Andres who implemented them, using gift culture and using the media to tell his story to the world. Karmic marketing started working for him in a big way.

Andres began to adapt this gift giving concept in a bigger way. He learned of a small clinic that was helping children who were recovering from AIDS. They had contracted it from their parents, who were drug addicts.

Andres gave the clinic the funds to rebuild their building and get some medicine. He did it from a karmic marketing approach. He gave without expecting return. The clinic told the media what was going on, and unbeknownst to Andres, his business exploded. Shortly after that contribution, he got a real estate deal for ten or eleven times what he had given to the clinic.

This story was so powerful that I helped Andres write his book. It's called *Homeless to Billionaire*, and I would add it to everybody's reading list. It talks about giving and his insights into business and attracting wealth.

Let me continue with eight basic principles for getting publicity.

Eight Publicity Principles

1. Word of mouth is the best publicity.
2. Link your message to the big news of the day.
3. Toot your own horn.
4. Timing is everything.
5. Don't be old news.
6. Be prepared for the impact of your promotions.
7. Keep your efforts coming.
8. Be nice.

The first one is, word of mouth is the best publicity. Give people something to talk about, because if you do, they're going to do the work for you. That's what flamboyant figures like Barnum and Houdini did. Houdini would hang upside down from a crane high in the air in a straitjacket and escape from it in front of the crowd below. He was giving people something to talk about.

Obviously, you don't need to get into a straitjacket or hang upside down. But you do want people to be talking about your product, service, or business. I have found that when you implement karmic marketing, people start to automatically talk about it, because they feel good about you and what you're doing.

When I came out with an album called *The Healing Song*, I gave one of the most powerful songs away. I had issued a news release and said that if you went to my site, you could listen to the song, which was a combination of hypnosis and relaxation, with a message of healing in it. They could download it for free.

This got people talking, because the song was a particularly great one, and they wanted others to know about it. Whenever you can get people to talk, that word of mouth is a grass fire movement.

Let me tell you a side story that illustrates many of these principles. Right before the pandemic hit, I was going to put on a live Master Mind group in San Antonio. I got together with my partner, Sean Donahoe, and we rented a hotel room. It would hold about fifty people, which is what I wanted; I wanted a tight group. We were going to charge quite a bit of money for it, but participants would have one-on-ones with me and Sean. It would be a live, in-person event.

As we were signing agreements and starting to do the publicity, the pandemic hit. People who had registered started to cancel, and people who had flights were canceling them. We couldn't get anybody to go. We didn't know how long the pandemic was going to last, so it became clear that a live event was not going to happen.

I looked at everything and thought, "One of my operating beliefs is there's always a way. If we can't do the live event, maybe we can do it virtually. Let's do an online event." I announced that there was going to be a virtual

Master Mind, and instead of only accepting fifty people, it would be unlimited, because it was being held online. Zoom was going to allow as many people as we could get into the virtual room.

We decided to do a virtual Master Mind live online for an unlimited amount of people, and we decided to charge a couple hundred dollars for it rather than thousands. We announced the virtual event, sent out the news releases, did the social media, but nobody signed up. Not a single person.

"What is going on?" I wondered. "Why is this not working?" I have learned that what looks like a mistake is actually information. It's feedback. As I looked at the feedback, I thought, "We can't do the live event, and we can't do the virtual one either. What do I do?"

My operating belief is there's always a way. We decided we were still going to do the event online, but for free. I announced it to social media, to my list, to the world.

In the end, 30,000 people attended this free, live, online event. We joyfully gave. I had guest speakers: my partner Lisa Winston, Sean Donahoe, and Chuck Pennington, and of course I spoke several times during the event.

We did this program from morning to night. People sat in front of their computers. People from all over the world ate their breakfast, lunch, and dinner with us. We didn't hold back, and we didn't sell anything. We joyfully gave, and we loved it. This was pure karmic marketing. After the dust settled, we sent out an offer to buy some of the audio and video recordings of the event, and we made several thousand dollars.

Rule number two is, link your message to a big story of the day. We linked our online event to the pandemic, because it was not only the big story of the day, it was the big story for a long time to come.

Rule number three: toot your own horn. If you don't tell people what you've done, they will never know. Many people believe the old adage that if you build a better mousetrap, the world will beat a path to your door. That's a belief. It is not a fact. It is not truth. You actually have to stir publicity. You have to plant some seeds with publicity because if you don't, nobody's going to know and nobody's going to buy.

In 2005 when my book *The Attractor Factor* was coming out, I wanted it to do well. I believed in my book, and I really wanted people to buy it, read it, and benefit from it. You don't want to get publicity to brag. You want to get publicity because you believe in something you're doing. I believed in my book. I wasn't famous at the time. I did have some Internet copywriter celebrity status, but the world didn't know who I was.

I wanted the world to know about my book, so I started writing news releases, and I started getting creative. I looked at the big news of the day, which was a new Harry

Potter book that was coming out. It was already number one on Amazon, even though it hadn't been printed yet. The pope had written a book, and it was number two.

I thought, "Now how in the world is my book going to beat Harry Potter and the pope?" Then I thought, "I'm really by myself. I'm an underdog here. It's me going up against empires—a media empire behind Harry Potter and a religious empire behind the pope—and here I am, this little guy in Texas with his computer.

"That's the story," I decided. I issued news releases that said, "Underdog author goes up against the wizard and the Pope." It was all about the fact that I had written this book, *The Attractor Factor*, and I was trying to stir the masses to pay attention to it while Harry Potter and the pope were out there and easily getting attention.

I kept sending out the news release, because I thought the angle was good. It wasn't about tooting my horn; it was about tooting the book's horn.

Remember rule number two about linking your story to the current message of the day. Harry Potter and the pope were current. I wanted to get in on that flow, and my news release did it. *The Attractor Factor* became the number one Amazon best seller in all categories. It beat Harry Potter, it beat the pope, and it brought notoriety to my book and me. Rhonda Byrne in Australia picked up a copy, read it, and thought, "I want this guy in my movie." And *The Secret* was filmed the next year.

Rule number four: timing is everything. We want to tie what we're doing to the current news. If we really want to use karmic marketing with publicity, we need to be paying attention to the top ten headlines and tie into them. We want to comment on the news, to leverage the news. That means you need to act on what's new right now. If you wait till tomorrow or next week, you will probably be considered old news.

That leads to rule number five: don't be old news. Nobody cares about old news. Timing is everything. Don't sit on your ideas. If you smell a fire brewing and you can attach yourself to it in some way, then by God, do it and do it today. Do it now.

Rule number six is, be prepared for the impact of your promotional efforts. It's all about the Boy Scout motto. Many years ago, I did a teleseminar, and we expected 1,000 people to attend. As it turned out, 12,000 people showed up, and all the lines collapsed. The Internet collapsed, our website collapsed, and it turned out to be a fiasco, because we lost the momentum and the potential for making money.

Of course, I've learned that there's no such thing as failure. It's all feedback. We did a campaign to regroup, correct, and prepare for more people on the next call. We just rescheduled the event and did it in an even bigger way.

A couple of decades ago, I had a client, Todd Barnhart, who wrote a book called *The Five Rituals of Wealth*.

He went on *Oprah*. Oprah asked him about the five rituals of wealth, and he explained them very well. It was great publicity, but she aired that episode before the book was published. Although everybody was excited, the book wasn't available yet. Todd told me afterwards that it was one of his big mistakes. He missed the avalanche. He missed the lotto win. He missed the big publicity moment.

If you're sending out news releases, if you're doing karmic marketing for your product or service, make sure you're prepared for orders. Make sure that when your phone rings, somebody answers. Make sure you have the product. Make sure shipping knows what to do, what orders to fulfill, and where they need to go.

Rule number seven is, don't stop now. Keep those press releases coming. One of the greatest secrets of success is persistence. Persistence beats out talent. It beats out luck. It beats our preparation. It beats out anything else you can bring up. Persistence.

The same thing is true with karmic marketing and getting publicity. Keep your stories going. Send them out on a regular basis. Don't just send fluff. Make sure you have a solid story. If you can send out one a week, or biweekly, do so.

Commit to befriending the media. I can't say it enough. It's the most underused marketing tool there is. When you combine it with karmic marketing and the other methods I've been talking about, the results could be staggering.

You can't just send one news release out. Send more, and do it on a regular basis. You'll create relationships with certain people in the media, and they'll look forward to hearing from you, but only if you start the ball rolling and keep the momentum up with persistence.

Rule number eight: Be nice. Say thank you. Media people are customers too. They're humans with human emotions. They like to be flattered. They like to be thanked. They like to be appreciated.

Think of all the things that you want in your own life. You want people to compliment you, acknowledge you, and thank you. Media people want the same thing. They might be doing a job, but behind that job is a person. Go back to Dale Carnegie's *How to Win Friends and Influence People*, another book that should be on everybody's reading list. It's a masterpiece, and in many ways it's common sense. It discusses all these things we're talking about with rule eight.

Be nice. Say thank you. Appreciate the media, and they will return the favor. It's a kind of psychological karmic marketing. If you give them the acknowledgment that they want and need, they in turn will give you attention. There you go—karmic marketing applied to publicity.

Some say that any publicity is good publicity. This is particularly true of those who do outrageous things to get attention online and in social media, even if they fall outside the boundaries of what most people would accept as moral or fair.

I say, throw that old idea out the window. Drive down the road, back up, and run over it. This is not what I'm talking about with karmic marketing. We don't want publicity for publicity's sake. We're coming from a spiritual place, a heart-centered place. What I want people to do with karmic marketing is share their love, their passion, their sincere story of why they're doing what they're doing.

There's a show on Netflix that I love. It's called *The Kindness Diaries*. It's a reality show about a man, Leon Logothetis, who decided to travel around the country living only on people's kindness. He did not accept money. He couldn't eat unless somebody gave him food. He could not sleep anywhere except in his car unless somebody gave him a place to lie down. He could not fill his car with gas unless somebody filled the tank for him.

Leon Logothetis traveled on the premise that people are kind and that he would survive, prosper, and thrive on the kindness of strangers. What people didn't know is that he's independently wealthy. Whenever he came across somebody that touched him, he would ask them what they needed to fulfill their dream, and he would give it to them.

I watched *The Kindness Diaries*, and I thought, "Look at the publicity he's getting." Look at how I'm talking about his show right now in this book. For a very long time to come, people around the world will be hearing about *The Kindness Diaries* and watching it.

The publicity Leon Logothetis is getting is amazing. What he's doing is sincere; it's coming from his heart. I am not endorsing publicity for publicity's sake. I'm not endorsing getting bad publicity. I'm endorsing love in business, in life, and in all relationships. That's the essence of karmic marketing.

7

Internet Marketing, Websites, Email, and Social Media

In this chapter, I want to go specifically into some practical, real-world strategies for putting karmic marketing into action.

These days, the action is for the most part on the Internet. Let me show why karmic marketing is the best type of marketing method for the Internet.

The Internet already has a gift culture mentality, meaning that people download (and expect) information for free. They're looking around for coupons to get things for free. *Free* is driving the Internet.

In some ways, the Internet is nothing more than a giant library. I think I've done well on the Internet partly because I used to live in the public library. In the old days, you had to go to a card catalog, pull out an index card, and write down the call number. Then you'd have to go up two or three flights to get a book, pull it off the shelf, and start reading it. The Internet, of course, reduces all of that to about a second.

In any event, since the beginning of the Internet, people have expected most things to be free. Karmic marketing slides into this world of giveaways and freebees. People are giving things away, but they don't know karmic marketing; they don't have its spirit or soul, and they don't know how to clear their beliefs.

As a result, most of the people out there are simply giving away things for free. Much of it is not very useful. Much of it is superficial. Much of it is garbage. But there's a whole lot of giving going on, and because of the nature of the Internet, people expect it.

One way of doing karmic marketing on the Internet is to make your website hypnotic—captivating. The research shows that most people don't stay longer than three seconds on a site. They go to it, they make a snap decision, and they are gone. Why? They weren't engaged. There wasn't anything to make them want to stay, to make them eager to know more.

We need to create a hypnotic website. We need to create attractions that will not only bring people there but hold them there long enough to get your message across.

That starts with great headlines: headlines with quotation marks, hinting at dialogue; headlines that provoke curiosity; excerpts from testimonials.

Headlines are only the beginning. We live in a world of high graphics. People like movement—video. I have found that video is the most captivating thing you can put on a website. I've been creating original video content for years now and posting it for free on Instagram, Facebook, and Twitter. As new forms of social media come around, I'll probably take my material there too.

Why am I posting video? I have found through my own testing that if I put up a text message, say an inspiring quote, I'll get some people to notice. If I put a photo up—of my dog, my partner, Lisa Winston, and me, or me with one of my new books—I'll get more likes than I will for the text message alone. I've also learned that if I put a video up, it will get far more attention, far more likes, far more engagement—thousands more—than mere graphics or text.

I discovered this when I was in Italy a few years ago, where Lisa and I spent thirty days vacationing. We were in farm country in a nice little villa near Lake Como, outside of Bellagio. Outside the villa one morning there was a chicken digging in the dirt. For whatever reason, I got my video camera and filmed it for about forty seconds, even though it didn't do anything other than stand there and dig in the dirt.

I took that forty-second video, and as an experiment I posted it on Instagram, Facebook, and Twitter. I thought it would just be a joke, but I wanted to find out if anybody would look. To my amazement, thousands of people watched the chicken digging in the dirt. At first I thought, "Boy, people must not have anything to do if they're watching a chicken in the dirt in Italy."

Then I thought, "Wait a minute. They're watching video. They want video." From that point on, I started to shoot more video and of course made it far more interesting than a chicken in the dirt. I've hired a young man in Ireland—Callum Rawling is his name—to make videos that I can post on Instagram, Twitter, and Facebook. These are collages and edited pieces from live talks, presentations, and radio and TV interviews. I'm astonished at how much research he does, and he puts them together into little stories.

These are videos about me and what I'm doing. One is about being stuck in the London airport when it closed because of weather and other problems. They evacuated the airport, so I and everybody else were standing outside in the winter. I had just come from Thailand, so I had no winter clothes. Everybody was scrambling to find a ride and a place to stay for the night.

I shared that experience. I shared that I'm human too. Not everything goes the way you want or expect, and you have to adapt. I also shared when I was going through a divorce that was not as easy or as pleasant as I thought it might be. I was sharing what some people might call my weakness, but it was also my humanness.

All of these things could be on a website. You don't have to put them all up, of course, but your site should be engaging and hypnotic.

From a karmic marketing standpoint, there should be something on your website besides your headline and your video that is free. Because you're building a business here, most of the time you're going to do what I *didn't* do with *Spiritual Marketing*: ask people for their names and email addresses. Put them on your mailing list. It will ultimately end up being your gold mine. You'll build a relationship with the people on this list, and they're the ones that are going to buy from you.

To begin this process, you implement karmic marketing. You give something away. Let me say something really important here: whatever you give should be something people would be willing to pay for. Too many people are giving away fluff. They're not giving away anything truly useful. They're teasing people.

Give away the farm. Give away what you would otherwise want to sell. If you give something that you would sell, you know it has value, and so does the person who gets it for free. They will feel it, they will remember it, they will use it, and they will stay with you.

Let's go on to email, because I want to illustrate a couple of key principles. One is the idea that we're building a relationship. That's the only way you succeed in life. Everything you want comes through other people. You want money? It's going to come from other people. You want some sort of product or service? It's coming through other people.

That means relationship. The essence of karmic marketing is relationship with other people. It's a relationship with the universe, with the cosmos, if you will.

When we create a newsletter or an email, we want to keep in mind that we're communicating with a real person, and we're creating a real relationship.

Let me tell you one of my secrets. When I write an email, I pretend that I'm writing to only one person. I take out of my mind the idea that this is going to go out as an all-encompassing email potentially reaching hundreds of thousands of people. That thought disconnects me from relationship. It makes me break rapport with the people who receive it.

However, if I pretend that I'm writing this email to one person only, it's going to create a natural rapport. It's going to be personal. It will seem as if it's Joe talking to you, and that I haven't sent it to anybody else—only to you. In the early days when I was practicing this hypnotic writing approach, some people wrote back and said, "Did you send this to anybody else?" They actually felt they were the only ones I was talking to.

In addition to the benefits I've mentioned, this technique creates a relationship. The person receiving it feels, "I know Joe Vitale. This is a real person. He is sincere."

Another thing that I do is stay in contact. It's not unlike me to email virtually every day to my list. They're not all sales messages, nor are they all free information. They're a balance of both. On one day, I might tell the story of meeting Andres Pira when I was in Thailand and what I learned from him. I'm not selling anything; it's as if I just came back from Thailand.

It's only a story, but it possibly teaches a message, hopefully inspiring the person, but not selling anything. I'm deepening the relationship. The next email might be more sales oriented: "Remember the guy in Thailand that I told you about? His name is Andres Pira. I helped him write a book. It's called *Homeless to Billionaire*, and it's now on Amazon. You're going to want to get it, because he reveals fourteen principles that took him from being nothing and nobody to being a charismatic young billionaire."

I have a balance between information and selling in order to make it seem that Joe's not just out for a buck, nor is he just spending all his time giving us things to do or to read. And ultimately, well, we kind of like Joe.

There's a rule in sales and marketing that people like to buy from people they know, like, and trust. I practice karmic marketing, share myself sincerely, and give people a window into my life; then I follow up later and say, "I've got a megaexpensive package, but here's why it's worth it." At this point, people have already learned to trust, like, and respect me. Now possibly they'll buy from me.

Today people sign up on an email list and suddenly get twenty other emails. It's obvious to them that the organization has sold their names. I'm not in favor of this practice. I believe that the key words here are *trust* and *respect* and *sincerity*. If we get somebody to sign up on our email list, it would betray that trust to turn around and sell it to somebody whom this person doesn't know at all. For me, this is insincere. It's not building trust or rapport.

Under the box that says, "Put your name and address here, and I will send you my free report," I add, "I will never sell or share your name, address, or anything. This is locked in my own vault." That way I'm at least conveying to people that you can trust me. If I do sell their email address, I lose trust, I lose business, and it's going to take quite a bit to rebuild it.

Let me move on to one of today's most significant marketing platforms: social media. In this arena, I am still learning, still experimenting. That's probably the case for everybody that wants to go into social media. Truth is, I don't know that any of us knows what works right now or all the time, although the basic principles—karmic marketing, starting the relationship by giving something for free, using video, being relevant, being consistent—are probably ones that we should always honor.

I've already emphasized how engaging video is. Whether it is on Twitter, Facebook, TikTok, or any of the other platforms that may be coming down the pipe, I believe that video is going to be the most engaging medium in the foreseeable future.

At the same time, we don't want to throw just any video up there. My story about the chicken in Italy was more or less a joke. Everything I post now is relevant to me, my message, and my audience. I want to post something that is inspiring, motivational, and spiritual, because those are the things that my target audience expects of me. I need to be thinking, "OK, they want to know more about awakening. They want to know more about prosperity consciousness. They want to know more about the background of my various books. They want to know more about how the law of attraction actually works." The videos that I create and post are all on those subjects, because they are what my audience wants to hear about.

We want to keep these principles in mind as we implement karmic marketing across the board, no matter what the social media platform is. We want to be relevant. We want to be consistent. We want to be persistent. I think we will want to be video based for a long time until something that I can't even imagine is created.

As I mentioned, I've been posting videos on social media for years. There was one that got 20,000 views. This was early on, when I was just starting on Instagram and barely had any followers at all. I was posting reluctantly, because I thought, "What is social media? It's just another thing I have to do. Is it going to help my business?"

But I started experimenting. Then one day I was just inspired. It was early in my divorce, and my divorce was not easy, so I was not sleeping well. My new partner, Lisa, developed Lyme disease, and I was taking care of her. During this period my father died, so I was also grieving while taking care of my new love while going through a divorce.

There was a lot going on. I wasn't sleeping, and it showed. There were dark rings under my eyes. But I felt inspired to make this video. I didn't have a studio. I was in a one-bedroom apartment with Lisa. I sat on the side of the bed in the apartment with my cellphone camera aimed at me. I looked at the camera, and in one minute, I talked about the three rules of using your brain to attract the results you want. I called it the three-day rule. I made that one-minute video, posted it on Instagram, and basically forgot about it. I just went about my business.

When I checked, I saw that 20,000 people had looked at it. I didn't have 20,000 followers, and most of my previous videos had attracted one or two thousand people. I wondered, "How did this happen?" I started to think about this, and asked some of my peers. What could have worked here? What made this stand out?

I think there were several elements. One of them was authenticity. I did not hide the fact that I was suffering. People wrote and said, "I see the sadness in your eyes." I thought, "Oh, my God. I love my people. I love my list. These people care. They're looking closely enough to know that I'm going through an unhappy period."

Many people also said, "I love the three-day rule. Please expand on it." The three-day rule ended up as a content piece that resonated with people. I also realized that the fact that I sat on the side of the bed doing this homemade video let people know how authentic it was. I wasn't in a studio. I didn't have a green screen behind me. I wasn't using professional engineers or photographers. This was raw. This was human. This was real. This was sincere. And I was practicing karmic marketing, because in that one minute I gave truly helpful advice.

I still stand by the three-day rule. Over time, I created a product around it, and I'm going to release a book on it. But that one-minute video worked because of elements that I didn't even know were at play.

8
Karmic Marketing and the Future

At this point we can ask, is karmic marketing the wave of the future?

I hope it will be, because it's based on love, respect, trust, and faith. It's based on the idea that your giving makes a difference not only to the recipient, but instantaneously to you. It's an action that comes back to you. You've entered a circulation of prosperity. It returns full circle and is multiplied, because it picks up riches along the way, comes back, and gives them to you again. In turn, you keep the cycle going by practicing love, respect, and trust and by giving more to your source of spiritual nourishment. That again goes back out into circulation.

My hope for the future is that karmic marketing will be practiced by businesses big and small, by entrepreneurs, and by individuals who aren't in business at all; they're just practicing because it's good karma. It can become a way of life. That's what I'm rooting for.

Sometimes there are competitors or even dishonest customers who will obscure the truth about you or your products or services. We see this challenge developing in different areas, particularly on social media. Even if you practice karmic marketing and are as honest and transparent as possible, there may be dishonest players that try to distort that truth.

Of course, I've run into that problem in my life online and off. Some of that took place in my divorce, and I had to look for relief and understanding.

What helped me? The ancient Stoics, going back to Seneca, Marcus Aurelius, and Epictetus. Marcus Aurelius, the Roman emperor, is the poster boy for Stoicism. He wrote a little book called *Meditations* for himself. He wrote down certain observations to remind himself of how to behave as an emperor, as a leader, as a man who was an influencer beyond belief. It was never intended for anybody else to read, but over time it's been published and republished, and it offers great insights. One that helped me especially was the idea that it does not matter what other people say and do; it matters what *I* say and do.

Your focus needs to be on you. You practice karmic marketing, giving, and heart-centered business. If there are naysayers and critics, if there are people on social media who try to twist the good you're doing into something bad, so be it. You let them live their lives. You live yours. P. T. Barnum said, "We can't all see alike, but we can all do good."

When I've been reminded of Gandhi, Martin Luther King, John F. Kennedy, or Robert Kennedy—any of these leaders that were trying to make a difference but hit opposition and in some cases were killed for their beliefs—I realize that they were living their calling. They were living their truth. They were living with sincerity. They were living from their heart, and they were living what they believed was right, no matter what anybody else said or did.

I've also concluded that nobody is going to understand my motivations, because those people are not inside me, any more than I can understand yours or anyone else's motivations. I'm not inside their brain or their personality. I don't know their true motives, and they don't know mine.

Marcus Aurelius, Seneca, and the gang are all saying, "What's really important is to do good." From that standpoint, I'm saying practice your karmic marketing and all the principles you believe in, and let the world say whatever it wants. The only thing that matters is what you say and do.

Another question about the future has to do with technology: an increasingly global market, artificial intelligence, increased personalization of products, and 3D printing. People speculate on how these innovations will affect marketing strategies.

Personally, I love technology. I'm a gadget guy. I'm always looking for the new apps, the new electronic toys that are coming out. From a karmic marketing standpoint, I know that we will adopt and use whatever the new whizbang device that come out. This has been true throughout time. P. T. Barnum used the newspapers because they were what was available. He was into technology, and he was curious about what was coming. He had one of the first phones. If he were here today, he would be using the Internet; he'd be using artificial intelligence.

To me, karmic marketing is a principle that can be implemented in any number of ways; it doesn't matter what new technology will show up in the future. Technology will not stop karmic marketing. It will, however, probably make it speedier in delivery and more pinpointed in directing the material to whoever would benefit the most.

I am excited about the future. I'm excited to see what we create. Who's sitting in their room right now, playing with wires and programming and coming up with something that no one else sees at this moment?

None of us really knows what the future holds. We like to think we have a handle on it, but we don't. We need to be in the moment, alert, and aware, and have an eye on what we want to create. I think it's far more important to practice certain principles that ensure a greater future. Doing karmic marketing right now is creating a promise of a future that is ten times more financially rewarding. When we implement karmic marketing today, we are creating a future that is prosperous, no matter what the changes and challenges happen to be.

In fact, because of the way karmic marketing works, what comes back to us comes back in surprising ways. If the future changes because of technology or some unforeseeable surprise, karmic marketing will adapt to it and give us our return through that change.

Karmic marketing is kind of an insurance policy. We don't really have to fear the future or worry about change. There's certainly going to be a future, and there's certainly going to be change. But with karmic marketing, we're taking care of now, we're getting the immediate, instant reward, and we're going into circulation, meaning that our reward going to come back ten times greater in the future, no matter what the future looks like.

For all people who are looking to start a career, start a new business, or change course in midcareer, I would quote Theodore Roosevelt, who said, "Do what you can with what you have right where you are."

I think that's wise on many levels. Begin whatever your passion is—your product, idea, or service. Do what you can with what you have right where you are. Get the momentum going. Start the engine. Move forward.

What business can best use karmic marketing right now? There's only one answer: all of them. There is no exception or exclusion. Anyone can do karmic marketing. It doesn't matter if you are a one-person business, an entrepreneur, or, like Andres Pira, you've got twenty businesses and you're a billionaire. Even if you only picked up this material out of curiosity, you can do it too. Karmic marketing works for everybody across the board. It is a law that has already been tested and proved.

Let me sum up the essence of karmic marketing with a story. In Houston back in the 1980s, I was working for an oil company. Every day at lunch, everybody got in their cars and they drove to the local mall, went to the food court, and got something to eat. One day, I got in my car and started driving to the mall. I got to a stop sign, and something in me said, "Turn left." Usually I never turned left, but this time I did. I followed my intuition.

I turned left, and within two blocks, on the left was an Italian deli. I was born and raised in Ohio. I grew up on Italian food and did not find any authentic Italian food anywhere in my area of Houston. And here was an Italian deli a couple blocks from where I was working.

I went into the deli and found a little man from Italy. His shop had authentic meats and cheeses from Italy. He offered to make a sandwich, and he did. I took it back to the office, because I didn't have time to eat it there.

As I ate the sandwich, tears came to my eyes. It was an authentic Italian deli sandwich. It brought me back to my childhood in Ohio and to my family.

I called up the owner, and I could tell when he answered that he expected me to complain. I said, "No, no. I'm calling because I want to thank you. This is the greatest sandwich I've had since I left my family. I'm just in awe."

He said, "Thank you," and hung up.

I thought, "He doesn't get it. He doesn't know how grateful I am."

I had his menu with me. I shut the door to my office, rewrote his menu, and used the company machine to copy it. I made 500 copies of it on nice, colored paper.

I went around and posted the flyer on every bulletin board in that building and the other buildings in the area, and I didn't think anything of it. But I did go to the deli the next day, because I wanted another sandwich, and found a line coming out of it, and there's no place to park.

I found a place to park, got out, and walked over. The owner met me at the door, and he was crying. He said, "I can't believe what you've done. All these people, they brought in a menu I never saw before."

"Well, it's your menu. I rewrote it."

"You hung it up on walls in the offices?"

"Yes," I said, "and that's not all."

Then I showed him the box of 500 flyers and gave it to him. He was beside himself, but he had to run back in because of all the people standing in line, waiting to place their orders, almost all of them from the company I was working for. I sat down and waited my turn.

For the next year, I didn't pay for any of my lunches. He fed me anything I wanted. He would make special meals for me. When my father and mother drove down from Ohio, I took them to the deli. The owner rolled out the red carpet and made some of the most exquisite delicacies of all time. He stuffed a chicken with cheeses and meats, and it was amazing. He spent most of the day doing it. He didn't charge us.

As time went on and I got to know the owner better and he got to know me and my struggles and dreams, he realized that I wanted to buy a house. I was living in a dump with my first wife. We were struggling. I was working, but I wasn't making enough money and didn't have enough credit history to buy a house.

The owner had his house built for him, and he had made it important to him by bringing things from Italy and putting them in the house. He had raised his family there, but he decided to buy another house.

This man gave me his house. As I remember this, I'm almost in tears. I gave with no expectation of return.

When I ate that sandwich, I wanted to show him I was grateful. I didn't have the term *karmic marketing* back then, and I didn't really understand the power of giving. I just knew I wanted to give. I was giving from my heart, because I was truly moved by this man and his food, and it awoke so many memories in me.

This man took care of me by not charging me anything. He took care of my parents when they came to visit, which they talked about till their death. They loved him, they loved that meal, and they loved the personalized service. My wife and I did move into his home, and we stayed there until her death.

This story illustrates virtually every principle of karmic marketing. When I gave, there was no expectation of return, because I didn't know what it would be. I didn't think it would be free lunches, and I certainly in my wildest imaginations never thought it would be a house.

I don't even know how to add a P.S. to that story, but I think one of the basic principles was genuine love, genuine gratitude, and genuine giving, and when it came to receiving, I genuinely received.

In conclusion, I would like to suggest a way to expect positive things in your life. A lot of people out there say, "Crap happens," or various versions of that. What I like to say is, "Expect miracles." Practice karmic marketing, and expect miracles.

About the Author

D r. Joe Vitale is a globally famous author, marketing guru, movie, TV, and radio personality, musician, and one of the top 50 inspirational speakers in the world.

His many bestselling books include *The Attractor Factor*, *Attract Money Now*, *Zero Limits*, *The Miracle: Six Steps to Enlightenment*, and *Anything Is Possible*.

He's also recorded numerous bestselling audio programs, from The Missing Secret and The Zero Point to The Power of Outrageousness Marketing and The Awakening Course.

A popular, leading expert on the law of attraction in many hit movies, including The Secret, Dr. Vitale discovered the "missing secret" not revealed in the movie. He's been on Larry King Live, Donny Deutsch's "The Big Idea," CNN, CNBC, CBS, ABC, Fox News: Fox & Friends and

Extra TV. He's also been featured in *The New York Times* and *Newsweek*.

One of his most recent accomplishments includes being the world's first self-help singer-songwriter as seen in 2012's *Rolling Stone Magazine*. To date, he has released seventeen albums! Several of his songs were recognized and nominated for the Posi Award, regarded as "The Grammys of Positive Music."

Well-known not only as a thinker, but as a healer, clearing people's subconscious minds of limiting beliefs, Dr. Joe Vitale is also an authentic practitioner of modern Ho'oponopono, certified Reiki healer, certified Chi Kung practitioner, certified Clinical Hypnotherapist, certified NLP practitioner, Ordained Minister, and Doctor of Metaphysical Science.

He is a seeker and a learner; once homeless, he has spent the last four decades learning how to master the powers that channel the pure creative energy of life without resistance, and created the Miracles Coaching® and Zero Limits Mastery® programs to help people achieve their life's purpose. He lives outside Austin, Texas, with his love, Lisa Winston.

His main site is www.MrFire.com.